The
5 Ingredient
Electric
Pressure
Cooker
Cookbook

The 5-Ingredient Electric Pressure Cooker Cookbook

EASY RECIPES FOR FAST AND DELICIOUS MEALS

Grace Ramirez

FOREWORD BY INGRID HOFFMANN, CHEF & AUTHOR
PHOTOGRAPHY BY HÉLÈNE DUJARDIN

ROCKRIDGE PRESS

For Grandma,
the secret ingredient in all of my dishes.

Contents

Foreword

WHEN GRACE ASKED ME to write the foreword for this book, I could not have been more excited and honored. I love Grace's food, and I love all things Grace. As I flip through the pages and take in the vivid photos, I feel Grace's energy, her vibrancy. I *see* her in these pages. I *hear* her voice. And best of all, I *feel* and *taste* her flavors. I'm certain that home chefs will be equally inspired by Grace's style and approachability, and make this cookbook their go-to for quick and creative meals.

Just like Grace, I grew up eating home-cooked meals, and I have distinct memories of the pressure cooker, not the least of which includes that familiar hissing sound. Thinking back, I can recall the wooden spoon that my mother would lay atop the pot and the lever moving up and down. From this, deliciously simple dishes like *carne en posta* and black beans, would emerge.

There is nothing better than the way food tastes and melts in your mouth when meals are cooked in a pressure cooker, especially when you factor in the convenience and ease of the appliance. It is probably the easiest way to consistently put nutritious food on the table. You simply add fresh whole-food ingredients, either frozen or room temperature, and in 20 minutes or less and with minimum preplanning, one can sit down and have a full meal. And let's not forget how budget friendly a pressure cooker can be! My mom used to say that it was much cheaper to feed an army with a bag of dried beans than having to buy five cans. And as we all know, mom is always right.

When it comes to one-pot kitchen appliances, I personally never really connected with the slow cooker as much as the pressure cooker, because there is much more effort that goes into slow cooking. To get the best flavors and to preserve the nutrients in the food, the best method, for me, is pressure cooking.

I understand that when it comes to safety, many people have their reservations with the traditional models. The iconic *hiss* is not only associated with delicious meals but also anxiety-inducing images of the top exploding. Enter modern technology and the rise of the multifunctional electric pressure cooker—the cooking game has officially changed. These modern appliances are 100% safe and quiet. There is no turning back to cooking any other way.

In *The 5-Ingredient Electric Pressure Cooker Cookbook*, Grace tests and takes the ease and versatility of the appliance one step further with five-ingredient recipes, proving why every kitchen should include this modern miracle. Not only do the recipes make you an expert and efficient user, but it saves the trouble of buying and storing an excess of ingredients that might not be used in the long run. As a professional chef, Grace combines her classic training with her passion for accessible ingredients and vibrant flavors to develop recipes that anyone can enjoy. The breakfast chapter is my favorite. One would not think to make the type of recipes that she has created, but she broadens the choices for the home chef, making it possible to turn out electric pressure cooking that is both easy and elevated.

—Ingrid Hoffmann
TV Host, Chef & Author

Introduction

JUST ABOUT EVERY MORNING of my childhood in Venezuela, I woke to the hiss of steam escaping from my grandparents' stove-top pressure cooker. It was my early-rising grandfather cooking food for the day, usually *carne mechada, asado negro,* or black beans, for a family of 10. My grandmother used the pressure cooker daily as well, to cook just about everything we ate.

Every now and then, a kitchen gadget comes along that has the ability to truly revolutionize the way people cook. The pressure cooker, invented in the seventeenth century and popularized after the Great Depression, was one of the first such devices. It changed the way people cooked by making it easier and quicker to get a meal on the table. My grandparents, like cooks all over Latin America, Europe, and the world, relied on their stove-top pressure cooker to prepare budget-friendly but tough meats and other long-cooking ingredients like dried beans, grains, and potatoes, turning them tender and delectable in a fraction of the time of traditional cooking methods.

I loved being in the kitchen when my grandparents were cooking. The enticing aromas of whatever was pressure-cooking filled the kitchen and made my mouth water. The meals that came out of that pressure cooker were flavorful and totally satisfying. But even though I loved my grandparents' cooking, there was always an undercurrent of fear when the pressure cooker was going. It could explode at any moment! At least, that's the way I remember it.

Today, cooks from all walks of life are rediscovering pressure cooking thanks to the introduction of supersafe, convenient, easy-to-use electric pressure cookers. These modern gadgets have numerous safety features, including automatic locking systems that don't allow you to open the pot until the pressure has been safely released. The latest models let you sauté or brown foods right in the pot and have built-in programs that turn them into rice cookers, slow cookers, yogurt makers, pasta boilers, and more. Perhaps best of all, they don't require "babysitting" the way the old-fashioned pressure cookers did. You can put your ingredients in the pot, seal the lid, turn the pot on, and walk away. You can even safely take a nap or leave the house to run errands or pick up the kids. When you come back, you'll be greeted with an intensely flavored, hot, ready-to-eat meal.

People of my grandparents' generation may still be using their trusty stove-top pressure cookers, but with electric pressure cookers, a whole new generation of cooks has embraced this quick and easy way of getting dinner on the table in the midst of their busy, connected lives. For me, personally, the electric pressure cooker has been life-changing. Of course, I use it for the traditional long-cooking dishes of my childhood—stews, rice, beans, and so on—but I've also been amazed to discover how many other things it can do well. You can cook pasta for a crowd right in the sauce, whip up a healthy and savory salmon dish in one minute, and steam or braise vegetables in no time. You can make a perfect risotto, *arroz con pollo*, or paella-style rice, and you don't have to stand there watching and stirring.

My mission as a chef is to encourage people not to be intimidated by cooking. This book is all about no-fuss, crowd-pleasing, nourishing food. To underscore just how easy it can be to make delicious and healthy meals in the electric pressure cooker, I've included only recipes with five or fewer ingredients (not including certain staples like salt, pepper, and other basic spices; flour; and oil). I have tested and retested these recipes to make sure that I've only included those that are super easy and super delicious. I guarantee that once you master a few of these recipes, you'll be forever in love with your electric pressure cooker. And once you've mastered all of the functions your electric pressure cooker offers, you won't have to worry about getting dinner on the table ever again.

Let's get started!

CHAPTER 1

The Revolutionary Electric Pressure Cooker

From its humble beginnings as an unwieldy cast-iron vessel, the pressure cooker has evolved over the past 200-plus years into a modern kitchen wonder. Today's electric pressure cookers are safe, user-friendly, and a joy to use.

The electric appliance is, simply put, one of the best things to happen to the home kitchen in decades. It offers everything the busy modern home cook needs in a cooking appliance—it's easy to use, economical, and versatile. Most importantly, it turns out nutritious, great-tasting meals quickly and without fuss! This chapter explains how the electric pressure cooker works and why it is beloved in modern kitchens worldwide.

SIX IMMEDIATE BENEFITS OF PRESSURE COOKING

I've been in love with pressure cooking ever since I was a little girl watching my grandmother cook with the stove-top version. When I discovered the electric pressure cooker, which is both safer and easier, I was instantly hooked. I could name countless reasons that I love this method of cooking, but here are my six favorite benefits of pressure cooking. The more you play around with the electric pressure cooker in your own kitchen, the more perks you're bound to discover.

Meals on the table fast. Pressure cooking can reduce cooking times by as much as 70 percent, making even traditionally long-cooking dishes like stews, stocks, beans, and grains quick enough to prepare after a busy workday.

Great meals made easy. Electric pressure cookers make it easy to cook delicious meals. With automatic pressure and timing functions, pressure cooking in an electric pressure cooker can be almost completely hands-off. You just put the ingredients in the pot, follow the timing guidelines, and let the pot do its thing.

Easy cleanup. The electric pressure cooker will make you a master of the one-pot meal. Many dishes can be made by literally tossing the ingredients in the pot and turning it on, while others can be pre-sautéed or browned right in the pot before pressure cooking. Either way, there's only one pot to clean!

Great flavor. The slow cooker has lured users with its promises of set-it-and-forget-it cooking, but there's one big drawback: The end result is usually not all that great. Flavors get muddled, meats dry out, liquids don't reduce into rich sauces. The pressure cooker solves many of these issues with quick cooking times that intensify flavors and tenderize meats and other foods, rather than simply cooking them to death. Using the sauté function, you can even reduce sauces right in the pressure-cooker pot before serving. The result is better-tasting food.

All-in-one functionality. Modern electric pressure cookers aren't one-trick ponies. They serve the functions of pressure cookers, slow cookers, rice cookers, and steamers. Some even make yogurt!

Conserve energy. With their fast cooking times, pressure cookers don't just save you time in meal prep; they also save you energy. Pressure cooking uses two to three times less energy than stove-top and other traditional cooking methods.

Preserve nutrients. With their shorter cooking times, pressure cookers help preserve the vitamins, minerals, and other nutrients in food.

INTRODUCTION TO ELECTRIC PRESSURE COOKERS

Invented in the seventeenth century, the pressure cooker—then a hulking cast-iron cooking vessel with a locking lid—uses the pressure of steam to raise the boiling point of water so that the water can get hotter before it turns into steam. The increased heat cooks food faster. This device got its first foothold as a common household appliance at the end of the Great Depression with the release of the Presto pressure cooker, the first saucepan-style stove-top pressure cooker with an interlocking lid. American housewives went crazy for them because they made cooking quicker and easier.

Then World War II put the kibosh on pressure cooker manufacturing, because the metals they were made from were needed for the war effort. Ironically, during this time, the need to limit the use of cooking fuel made the pressure cooker, with its greatly reduced cooking times, especially attractive. Unable to buy new pressure cookers, neighbors and friends had to share.

Once the war ended, there was a pent-up demand for new pressure cookers—which a slew of manufacturers rushed to fill, some by producing inexpensive and low-quality cookers made from stamped aluminum. Ultimately, these low-quality cookers, which were often ineffective and/or dangerous, sullied the appliance's reputation. The pressure cooker still had its die-hard fans, but many of the manufacturers went out of business or stopped making pressure cookers in favor of other, more profitable products.

In the 1970s, as more and more women began to work outside the home and quicker cooking methods were more in demand than ever, the pressure cooker got a boost as manufacturers gave them a style upgrade and developed a safer type of interlocking lid that reduced the risk of accidents. For the next couple of decades, the pressure cooker remained a tool in the dedicated cook's armory, but it still wasn't for everyone.

That is, not until the 1990s, when the electric pressure cooker was introduced, revolutionizing the cooking appliance that had revolutionized home cooking generations earlier. Like their stove-top counterparts, electric pressure cookers reduced cooking times and produced succulent roasts, stews, and other dishes in a fraction of the time it would take to cook using traditional methods. Giving them a leg up over the stove-top versions of old, electric pressure cookers are easy to operate, employing technology that allows you to pretty much set them to cook and walk away—no babysitting required!

One of the biggest concerns for consumers has always been safety. With built-in safety mechanisms, the newer electric pressure cookers are very safe. It's virtually impossible to open the cooker once the internal pressure has exceeded the outside pressure, which eliminates the risk of explosions. The electric pressure cooker made pressure cooking safer—no more worry about exploding pots!

With today's culture of extreme busyness—two-career households, single parents, and the constant juggling act of modern life—time-saving devices are a godsend. Even the busiest people still need to get dinner on the table every night, and more and more, we want it to be a healthy, nutritious dinner made from whole foods. The electric pressure cooker is a dream come true, making it possible to cook whole grains, dried beans, meats, and other foods in record time, often all in one pot for easy cleanup.

The electric pressure cookers available today go even further, offering a multitude of cooking options from basic pressure cooking (with high- and low-pressure options), to browning/sautéing right in the pot, steaming, slow cooking, and cooking rice and pasta. Some even make yogurt! With two pressure-release options—natural release and quick release—you can even control how quickly the pot depressurizes, which helps prevent some of the unintended ill effects of pressure cooking like chewy meat or overcooked vegetables.

With built-in safety features, temperature regulators, pressure-release valves, sensors, and timers, electric pressure cookers offer true convenience. Unlike stove-top pressure cookers, once you've put the ingredients in the pot, set your cooking method and time, and sealed the pot, you don't need to babysit to ensure that it doesn't explode, fail to come to pressure, or burn your meal.

Electric pressure cookers are available in a range of sizes, from mini 2-quart pots to 10-quart pots. The most common size is the 6-quart pot, so the recipes in this book are written for that size.

ELECTRIC PRESSURE COOKER GAME CHANGERS

Numerous companies make electric pressure cookers these days, and almost all of them offer multifunction versatility that lets you slow cook, pressure-cook, steam, sauté, simmer, reduce, cook rice, and even, in some cases, boil pasta or make yogurt. The best allow you to brown and sauté right in the pot, set to cook without constant monitoring, and manually adjust pressure and timing. And, of course, they're easy to use and easy to clean.

The four top-selling brands today are Cosori, Cuisinart, Power Pressure Cooker XL, and, perhaps the most famous, Instant Pot. These four brands score well on the points mentioned above, but each offers distinct advantages. Here I'm comparing the 6-quart models of each brand, all of which operate at a wattage of 1000.

Cosori Premium 6Qt Pressure Cooker includes multiple functions: Bake, Sauté and Brown, Boil, Steam, Slow Cook, and Pressure Cook (six different pressure levels). It can be used as a slow cooker, rice cooker, sauté pan, yogurt maker, hot pot, pasta pot, steamer, warmer, and pressure cooker. It uses a stainless-steel inner pot. At around $80, it's the most economical of the available electric pressure cookers.

Electric Pressure Cooker Comparisons

MAKE/MODEL	COSORI PREMIUM 6QT	CUISINART CPC-600	POWER PRESSURE COOKER XL 6QT	INSTANT POT DUO PLUS 60
Average price	$80	$98	$100	$130
Cooking pot material	Stainless steel	Nonstick-coated aluminum	Nonstick-coated aluminum	Stainless steel
Cook settings	6	5	3	9
Pressure settings	6	2	1	2
Preprogrammed cooking functions	17	0	8	14

Cuisinart CPC-600 includes settings for pressure cooking (two pressure settings), browning, simmering, sautéing, and warming. It has a coated nonstick inner pot. Priced at under $100, this is an economical choice.

Power Pressure Cooker XL 6 Quart offers multiple functions for pressure cooking (just one pressure setting), slow cooking, rice cooking, steaming, and so forth. It is the only one that offers a pressure-canning function. The inner pot is made of nonstick-coated aluminum. The price is in the middle of the price range at around $100.

Instant Pot Duo Plus 60 functions as a slow cooker, rice cooker, egg cooker, sautéer, steamer, warmer, yogurt maker, and sterilizer, and offers two pressure levels (low and high). The inner pot is made of 3-ply stainless steel. At around $130, this one is on the upper end of the price range, but many users find it to be worth the price. There is also a $150 "Ultra" model, which includes multiple temperature settings for sautéing and slow cooking and even more preprogrammed cooking modes.

The recipes in this book are universal enough for any of the listed electric pressure cookers, as well as other brands with similar functionality, but when relevant, I provide specific tips to convert the recipes for the particular features of these top 4 brands.

UNIVERSAL EASY SETTINGS

Each pressure cooker make/model has its own unique functions, but there are some universal settings that are common to all electric pressure cookers. Different makers may use slightly different terminology (e.g., *sear* vs. *brown*), but the functions are more or less the same. Here are the primary functions that you'll find on all electric slow cookers.

Manual or Pressure Cook The recipes in this book typically call for using the Manual/Pressure Cook button. Some cookers allow you to choose different pressure settings, but if yours only has one pressure setting, just use that when high pressure is called for. When using the pressure settings, make sure the steam valve is closed (or set to Sealing). The steam valve must be closed in order to build up the pressure inside the pot that this method requires.

Slow Cook Using this button turns your electric pressure cooker into a slow cooker. When using this setting, leave the steam valve open, since this setting doesn't bring the pot to pressure but rather cooks with low heat over a long period of time. The Slow Cook function can also be used to simmer ingredients slowly, either with the lid off or with the lid on and the steam valve open.

Sauté/Brown/Sear This function goes by different names, but the purpose is the same: to heat the pot and precook foods before pressure cooking, or to reduce sauces or broths after pressure cooking. Use it (with the lid off) to sear meats, brown onions, or sauté vegetables before sealing up the pot and pressure-cooking. If your pot gives you a choice between low, medium, and high sauté settings, use medium for sautéing and browning, and high for searing meats or reducing sauces.

Keep Warm Most electric pressure cookers automatically switch to the Keep Warm setting once the timed cooking function chosen has been completed. You can use the Keep Warm button to keep cooked foods warm until the rest of the meal is ready or to warm up dishes that have cooled.

Steam Designed for use with the included trivet or your own appropriately sized steam basket, the Steam function heats at full power continuously, boiling the water below and steaming the food above.

Off/Cancel This button turns the pressure cooker off. When the cooking function is completed, most cookers will automatically switch to the Keep Warm function, but you can also cancel and switch the machine off by using the Off/Cancel button. Note that pressure will be released faster if you switch off the Keep Warm function.

ELECTRIC PRESSURE COOKER FAQS

A generation ago, pressure cooking required a whole lot more knowledge and experience to get right. The new electric pressure cookers, though, make it easy to cook a wide range of dishes quickly, easily, and with little fuss. Here are answers to some of the most frequently asked questions about electric pressure cookers.

➺ How can I convert my favorite stove-top pressure cooker recipes for the electric pressure cooker?

Converting recipes written for stove-top pressure cookers to use in an electric pressure cooker requires minimal adjustments. Just use the Mannual/Pressure Cook button and set the time to whatever cooking time the original recipe calls for.

➺ How can I convert my favorite traditional recipes for the electric pressure cooker?

To convert a traditional recipe, first make sure you're using a recipe that's suitable for pressure cooking. Liquid is necessary to create steam inside the pot and build up the pressure, so things like beans, rice, and grains that normally cook in liquid make the most sense. Keep in mind, though, that liquid doesn't get cooked off like it does in traditional stove-top or oven recipes, so you won't need as much of it. In general, a pressure cooker needs a minimum of 1 cup of liquid to build up enough pressure, but if you're cooking something like meat or vegetables that contain a lot of water, you can add less, maybe ½ to ¾ cup of liquid.

To adjust the cooking time, look for pressure-cooker recipes for similar dishes. You can find cooking-time charts on page 147 or online that show appropriate cooking times for ingredients like meats, grains, dried beans, and vegetables. Usually the cooking time will be about half or two-thirds as long as it is in a traditional recipe. For instance, rice can be cooked in 8 minutes in the pressure cooker as opposed to 15 to 20 minutes on the stove top. A whole chicken that might take an hour and 15 minutes to roast in the oven cooks in about 25 minutes in the pressure cooker.

➥ How can I convert my favorite slow-cooker recipes for the electric pressure cooker?

Slow-cooker recipes are some of the easiest to repurpose for the electric pressure cooker; usually all you have to do is reduce the cooking time. A meat recipe that cooks for 8 hours on low or 4 hours on high in the slow cooker, such as a beef stew, requires only 30 to 35 minutes under high pressure. Likewise, a recipe that takes 6 hours on low or 3 hours on high in the slow cooker takes 20 to 25 minutes in a pressure cooker. Recipes that combine slow-cooking and quick-cooking ingredients (like meat and vegetables) can still work in the electric pressure cooker, but it's best to cook the meat first, stop the cooking 5 to 10 minutes before the end of the cooking time, release the pressure using a quick release, add the vegetables, and then cook for another 5 to 10 minutes.

➥ Should I use quick pressure release or natural pressure release?

Quick pressure release is when you open up the pressure cooker's release valve when the cooking time is completed, letting the steam out quickly, in about 2 minutes. *Natural pressure release* is when you don't touch the valve and instead let the pressure release naturally over time, which can take anywhere from 5 minutes to 30 minutes.

Once the pressure is fully released, the float valve (a small silver pin on the lid of your pressure cooker) will drop, allowing you to open the pot.

Both of these release methods are useful, depending on what you're cooking. When you're cooking ingredients that take a long time to cook (such as meat) or ingredients that might foam up as the steam releases (like beans or oats), natural release is the way to go. Natural release is also preferred for meats, because it allows the meat to relax, giving you a more tender final product.

Quick release, on the other hand, is ideal for faster-cooking ingredients like vegetables or fish, since the extra time from a natural release would overcook them.

Note that you can let the pressure release naturally for 5 or 10 minutes and then open up the valve and let the remaining pressure release quickly. Since the pressure will be lower by this time, foaming will be less of an issue.

➤➤ When a recipe calls for a cooking time of, say, 30 minutes, how long will it actually take from the time I turn on the pressure cooker until we can eat?

The cooking time refers to how long the dish needs to cook once the pot has come up to pressure. You'll notice that when you turn your pressure cooker on and set the timer for 30 minutes, it doesn't start counting down the time until after the float valve has popped up, indicating that pressure has been achieved. The time it takes for the pot to come up to pressure varies based on what you're cooking, how much food you're cooking, how much liquid is in the pot, etc. It can take anywhere from 5 to 30 minutes to achieve pressure and begin the cooking process. Similarly, once the pressure-cooking process is completed, it takes some time to release the pressure before you can open the pot. Pressure release can take anywhere from a minute or two for quick release to as long as 30 minutes for natural release. The total time, then, from when you seal up the pressure cooker and hit start to when you sit down to eat dinner can vary by an additional 15 to 60 minutes. One of the great benefits of electric pressure cookers, however, is that once the cooking time is completed, they automatically switch to Keep Warm and begin to release pressure naturally.

➤➤ What is the minimum volume of liquid that must be added to the pot?

A pressure cooker works by heating up liquid to create steam, which creates pressure. Most guides say that a minimum of 1 to 1½ cups of water are needed for an electric pressure cooker to work properly. Some ingredients, though, release a fair amount of liquid as they heat up, which contributes to the total volume of liquid in the pot. In my experience, you often only need to add ½ to 1 cup of liquid for proper pressure cooking. Some dishes with ingredients that contain a lot of water (like some fruits and vegetables) don't require any additional liquid to be added, while sauces or other food items with a high sugar content might need a little extra stock or other liquid to prevent burning during cooking. Until you get some experience cooking with your electric pressure cooker, it's best to follow recipe instructions, but with time, you'll begin to get your own sense of how much liquid you need to add.

➥ Can I put frozen foods in the pot to cook, or do I need to thaw them first?

Unlike with slow cookers, you can put frozen foods right in the pressure cooker. It may, however, take longer for the pot to come up to pressure and the cooking timer to begin to count down, so factor that into your timing.

➥ If I double a recipe, should I also double the cooking time?

No. The cooking time depends on the density of the ingredients, not the volume. If you simply double the quantity of ingredients, you shouldn't need to change the cooking time at all. It might take longer for the pot to come to pressure, but the actual cooking time will remain the same.

➥ Speaking of doubling the recipe, if I want to make twice as much, should I just double all the ingredients? What about halving a recipe?

Changing the volume of a recipe is a little trickier than just doubling or halving each of the ingredients. If you double a recipe by doubling all of the ingredients, including the added liquid, you might water down your finished dish. If the original recipe calls for ½ cup of liquid, for instance, ½ cup may be all that is needed even after you've doubled the other ingredients. That amount will probably still be enough for the pot to come up to pressure, so you're probably better off leaving it at ½ cup. Similarly, if you're halving a recipe, you may need to keep the liquid measurement the same. If a recipe calls for ½ cup of liquid, you'd still want to use ½ cup of liquid, since ¼ cup might not be enough to generate the steam needed to bring the pot up to pressure.

CHAPTER 2

The Electric Pressure Cooker Kitchen

One of the best things about cooking with an electric pressure cooker—that you just put your ingredients in, turn it on, and wait for the magical moment when your meal is ready to eat—is also the thing that makes it the most mysterious and, well, intimidating to many people. This chapter will detail everything you need to know to be able to put your faith in the pressure cooker, trusting that in the end, your meal will be just as delicious as you intended.

THE BEST FOODS FOR PRESSURE COOKING

Pressure cookers drastically reduce cooking times, which makes them ideal for foods that usually take a long time to cook. Here are the best foods to cook in your electric pressure cooker.

VEGETABLES

The best vegetables for electric pressure cooking are hardy vegetables that require long cooking times. Here are some of my favorites.

Potatoes Potatoes take a long time to become tender under normal cooking conditions (roasting, baking, boiling, or steaming). The pressure cooker turns all types of potatoes—including russets, baby potatoes, sweet potatoes, and yams—tender in a fraction of the time, making it a great way to prep potatoes for potato salad, mashed potatoes, and other potato dishes.

Artichokes Artichokes are a delicious treat and are loaded with antioxidants and fiber. The downside is that they take about 45 minutes to steam on the stove top—but in an electric pressure cooker, just 8 or 9 minutes on high pressure and a quick pressure release renders them perfectly tender. Including the time it takes to bring the pot up to pressure, they can be ready to go in under 20 minutes.

Beets Beets make a beautiful addition to salads or a lovely side dish on their own, but they can take up to 90 minutes to roast or steam. The electric pressure cooker makes quick work of them, though. Medium beets (3½ to 4 inches in diameter) cook in 20 to 25 minutes at high pressure with a quick pressure release.

Corn on the cob Corn on the cob is easy to steam or boil, but pressure cooking helps it retain more of its nutrients, and it is a bit quicker—plus you can cook many ears of corn at once in the electric pressure cooker. The key is to remember that the corn will begin cooking while the pot is heating up, so you need to be careful not to overcook it.

MEATS

Pressure cooking is a high-temperature cooking method, so it's best suited for meats that require a lot of cooking in order to become tender. When you want to pressure-cook meat, look for the least expensive, fattiest, most marbled types of meat. Meat on the bone is even better, since the bone helps lock in juices and add flavor.

Pork shoulder/butt Pork shoulder (also called pork butt) is a tough, fatty cut that's perfect for making stews and shredded- or pulled-pork dishes. Pressure-cooked with seasoning and a bit of liquid, this cut becomes fork-tender and perfect for soaking up barbecue sauce or other tasty marinades.

Pork ribs Barbecued pork ribs are a finger-licking treat, but normally the ribs have to be boiled or steamed on the stove top for an hour or more to make them tender before barbecuing. Precooking them in the electric pressure cooker is quicker and easier. Steam them on a rack with a bit of water in the pot. After about 25 minutes and a natural pressure release, they'll be fall-off-the-bone tender, ready to be eaten or doused with a delectable sauce.

Beef pot roast Beef roasts require long cooking times to become tender, so pressure cooking is a great method to use. Pot roast stays juicy, and all of the meat's flavor is trapped inside the cooker where it can't cook off, giving the cooking liquid great depth of flavor as well.

Stew meat Whether you're talking about beef, pork, or lamb, the toughest cuts are often sold as "stew meat." These require long cooking times, but when treated right, they deliver great flavor. With an electric pressure cooker, you can brown the meat right in the pot, add a bit of liquid and other ingredients, and cook at high pressure, all in roughly half the amount of time you'd need to cook it on the stove top.

CHICKEN

Chicken can be tricky in the pressure cooker. Different cuts vary in the amount of time they need to be pressure cooked, especially breasts. Bone-in and whole chickens tend to work better.

Whole chicken Cooking a chicken whole in an electric pressure cooker is a great way to get tender, moist, flavorful meat that's perfect for using in dishes like chilaquiles, pasta, or chicken salad. The moist environment prevents the usual problem of the white meat drying out and overcooking before the dark meat is done. Season your chicken heavily before cooking and put just about a cup of liquid (you can use water or broth) in the pot. Pull the meat off the bones and discard the skin, then put the bones back in the pot, cover with water, and make a delicious homemade chicken broth.

Bone-in thighs Chicken thighs are dark meat, which means they have more fat and won't dry out as quickly as white meat. I like to cook thighs on the bone since the bones add extra flavor, but I'll often remove the skins before cooking just to keep the fat content in check. I love to cook thighs and rice together in the pressure cooker (along with seasonings and veggies) for an easy one-pot meal.

Wings Like thighs, chicken wings are dark meat. They also have a high bone-to-meat ratio, and cooking meat on the bone infuses it with flavor. Chicken wings (with bones and

Trickier Foods for the Electric Pressure Cooker

The electric pressure cooker is a fantastic time-saver for busy cooks, but there are some foods that aren't as ideal as others. A good rule of thumb is that any food that cooks quickly via traditional methods (like thin, lean proteins with little to no fat) needs to be approached correctly for the pressure cooker.

Broccoli This healthy vegetable can be steamed to tender perfection in about 5 minutes, so there's really no reason to cook it in a pressure cooker. Plus, it will likely be overcooked before the pot fully pressurizes.

Boneless, skinless chicken breast Because chicken breast is very lean, the high-temperature cooking environment of the pressure cooker can dry it out and make the meat stringy. If you're cooking chicken breast in the pressure cooker, be sure to use larger, thicker chunks, brown it first, and use a short cooking time to prevent it from becoming too dry.

Lean steak Like chicken breast, lean beef will turn leathery when cooked at a pressure cooker's high temperature. Treat pricey cuts of beef right by cooking them on the stove top, in the oven, or on the grill. Save the pressure cooker for tenderizing inexpensive cuts of meat like brisket and pot roast.

Boneless pork chops Pork chops are quite lean, and if they're boneless they'll cook even faster than they would on the bone. As with steak, they'll likely be overcooked by the time the pot comes up to pressure.

Pork tenderloin This is another very lean cut of pork that tends to become overcooked and dry in the pressure cooker.

Delicate fish fillets Meatier, oilier fish like salmon does well in the pressure cooker, as long as you cook it at low pressure and for a very short time, but more delicate fish like sole or flounder is better off being seared in a skillet.

Crispy foods Pressure cooking requires liquid to create steam to build pressure. This means a pressure cooker is a moist cooking environment. Any foods that you want to end up with a crispy skin or outer shell are better off being fried in oil, seared in a skillet, or broiled or roasted in the oven.

Multiple ingredients with widely varying cooking times If you're cooking a dish that includes both long-cooking meat and quick-cooking vegetables together, you'll end up with either very undercooked meat or very overcooked vegetables. Instead, it's best to steam the vegetables in the microwave or on the stove top and then mix them in with the rest of the ingredients once the pressure cooking is complete. For quick-cooking foods like edamame and spinach, you can sauté them right in the inner pot once the other foods are done cooking.

Thick or sugary sauces Creamy, cheesy, or sugary sauces can stick to the bottom of the pot and scorch, so they're best made on the stove top where you can watch them carefully and stop their cooking quickly as needed.

skin) cook quickly in the pressure cooker and stay juicy and plump. To get a crispy skin, I suggest roasting in a hot oven after pressure cooking.

Whole bone-in, skin-on breasts Bone-in chicken breasts are a great choice for the pressure cooker, as they lock in moisture, cook slower than boneless cuts, and impart a lot of added flavor to the finished dish.

GRAINS AND LEGUMES

Grains and legumes (especially whole grains and dried beans) take a long time to cook on the stove top, so the pressure cooker is a great solution. For more details about grains and legumes, see Electric Pressure Cooking Time Charts (page 147).

Rice The best thing about cooking rice in an electric pressure cooker is that you can just put the rice and water in the pot, turn it on, and let it do its thing without babysitting it. You can do the same thing with a rice cooker, but the pressure cooker does it in a fraction of the time.

Steel-cut oats Cooked in the pressure cooker, steel-cut oats turn out creamy and tender in very little time. They make a great healthy breakfast topped with fruit and nuts.

Dried beans I always have dried beans in my pantry, but I can never seem to think of them the day before I want to cook them, in time to soak them overnight. The electric pressure cooker solves this problem! You can start with dried beans and be eating a delicious bean dish for dinner in less than 45 minutes. This works for most types of beans. I love using black beans, cannellini beans, or pinto beans.

Quinoa This healthy whole grain needs just 1 minute at high pressure to achieve a tender and perfectly edible texture.

KITCHEN SAFETY GUIDE

Electric pressure cookers are much safer than the stove-top pressure cookers of old, but there are still some safety tips to keep in mind to avoid pressure-cooking mishaps.

1. Always check to ensure that the bottom of the inner pot and the heating plate it sits on are clean and dry before turning on your pressure cooker.

2. Check that the float valve, steam-release valve, and antiblock shield are also clean and free of any food, and make sure the sealing ring is secure.

Common Mistakes

Once you've cooked a few recipes in your electric pressure cooker, you'll have a good sense of how it works and will understand just how easy pressure cooking can be. Though it's an easy-to-use appliance, there are some common mistakes people make when they first start using one.

Forgetting the sealing ring. I think every new electric pressure cooker user must make this mistake at least once: forgetting to put the sealing ring in the lid before closing the pot and turning the cooker on. Without that seal, the pot won't come up to pressure. If your pot has been on for a long time and isn't reaching full pressure, this is one of the first things to check for.

Forgetting to set the steam-release valve to the sealing position. If you don't set the valve to the sealing or sealed position, steam will escape, and the pot won't come up to pressure. If you see a lot of steam being released and the pot isn't coming up to pressure as quickly as you expected, check the position of the valve.

Putting quicker-cooking and slower-cooking ingredients in at the same time. Some ingredients—stew meats, for instance—take a long time to cook, even in the pressure cooker. Others, like many vegetables, cook very quickly. If you put a pot roast and carrots in the pot at the same time, your carrots will turn to mush long before the roast is cooked through. To avoid this, cook the longer-cooking ingredients under pressure until almost done, then release the pressure, add the quicker-cooking ingredients, and finish the cooking time.

Using too much liquid. The pressure cooker works by trapping steam, creating pressure, and raising the cooking temperature to make the cooking process faster. Because the steam is trapped inside rather than evaporating, you don't need much liquid at all. Using too much will water down your recipe, diluting the intense flavors the pressure cooker is famous for producing.

Using too little liquid. If there's too little liquid, the pressure cooker can't produce enough steam to achieve the pressure necessary to seal the pot. If you're cooking ingredients that release their own liquid, you only need to add about ½ cup, but if you're cooking dry ingredients, the minimum is more like 1 to 1½ cups.

Not using an insert. To prevent burning, many foods that are high in sugar or contain milk will need to be cooked in a separate dish instead of the pressure-cooker pot. Glass, metal, and ceramic baking dishes can all be used as inserts. A good rule of thumb for the recipes using an insert in this book is that the insert should be oven-safe and at least 2 inches deep.

3. When in use, always place the electric pressure cooker on your counter, not in an enclosed cabinet or with anything covering it.

4. Be careful not to overfill the cooking pot. When cooking starchy foods, foods that are likely to foam, or foods that will expand during cooking (like grains, beans, and bready foods), fill the pot only half full. For nonfoamy foods and foods that won't expand much during cooking, you can fill the pot up to three-quarters full, but no more.

5. Use caution when releasing the pressure. Use a silicone oven mitt or other protective covering when opening the steam-release valve, and always make sure to face the valve away from your face and body.

6. Unplug your electric pressure cooker when you're not using it.

CLEANING AND CARING FOR YOUR ELECTRIC PRESSURE COOKER

Electric pressure cookers are not only easy to use but also easy to clean. Follow these guidelines for easy care and cleaning of your electric pressure cooker.

1. Unplug your electric pressure cooker after use.

2. If the inner pot is dishwasher-safe, go ahead and put it in the dishwasher if you like. If it's not dishwasher-safe, use soap and water in the sink.

3. Remove the sealing ring or gasket from the lid after each use and wash it with soap and water or run it through the dishwasher. Be sure it's dry before replacing it in the lid. Note that the ring might absorb the scent of certain spices or other strong-smelling ingredients. Washing the ring with soap and water or running it through the dishwasher will help. Most people say that the smell doesn't transfer to other dishes cooked in the pot, but if this bothers you, you can always purchase a second ring to use for dishes without strong scents (like desserts).

4. Clean the lid with a damp sponge or cloth, but don't submerge it in water.

5. Remove the pressure-release valve and other removable parts for washing, and be sure to replace them once they're clean and dry.

THE GAME-CHANGING 5-INGREDIENT RECIPES

The recipes in this book are designed to be easy to make, whether you have previous experience with the electric pressure cooker or not. They're both familiar and inspired, but none of them require long lists of ingredients or arduous prepping and cooking processes. In fact, the recipes here use five or fewer ingredients (not counting certain basics—see below). Some of the recipes will be, say, more suitable for a family meal, or easier to get on the table quickly, so I've labeled each recipe as follows to help you plan ahead.

30 Minutes or Less These recipes take 30 minutes or less to prepare from start to finish (including prep time, time to bring the pot to pressure, cook time, and release time). These recipes use a combination of pantry staples and fresh ingredients from your weekly shopping trip.

Quick Prep These recipes can be in your pressure cooker and ready to start cooking in 5 minutes or less.

Family Friendly These recipes serve 4 or more people.

Kid Friendly These recipes use kid-friendly ingredients, so they're perfect for all ages.

Easy Weekend These are recipes that are easy to make but will take 45 minutes or longer to prepare from start to finish. Some of these recipes also use seasonal ingredients and/or special ingredients that may require a bit of a splurge.

BASIC ESSENTIAL INGREDIENTS

The recipes in this book all use five or fewer ingredients, not counting certain basic staples that most people already have in their fridge, pantry, or spice rack. These include:

- **Oil** I use canola oil, olive oil, and coconut oil in my recipes. If you don't have coconut oil, any neutral-flavored, high-smoke-point oil (like safflower, sunflower seed, or grapeseed) will do. Cooking spray oil is also fine.

- **Butter** Many of my recipes use butter, but you can substitute olive oil or coconut oil if you prefer to avoid dairy products.

- **Salt** Choose an additive-free salt like kosher salt or sea salt.

- **Pepper** Opt for freshly ground black pepper for the best flavor.

- **Vanilla Extract** This kitchen staple is a subtle enhancement to most baked goods and cooking.

- **Stock** It's easy to keep a quart or two of store-bought stock in the pantry. Or, make delicious stock stocks from this book—such as Chicken Stock (page 134), Fish Stock (page 135), or Vegetable Stock (page 136)—and store in the freezer.

- **Garlic** I use a lot of fresh garlic in my recipes, so I recommend always keeping a bulb around.

- **Onions** The majority of the recipes in this book begin with diced or sliced onions. You can use white or yellow onions. If you don't have either of those but do have shallots or red onions, feel free to substitute.

- **Flour** This is a classic kitchen staple and comes in handy when you need to thicken soups or stews or make a roux.

Huevos Rancheros Casserole, *page 24*

CHAPTER 3

Breakfast

When you think of pressure cooking, you probably think first of big, savory stews and soups. But the electric pressure cooker makes great breakfasts, too! I especially love to use mine to make brunch for friends. It makes it really easy to cook things like Huevos Rancheros Casserole (page 24) or Challah Bread Pudding (page 37) for a crowd. It's also perfect for making oatmeal, porridge, and other hot cereals.

Popular electric pressure cookers often have settings or pre-programmed cooking functions set up specifically for breakfast foods. The Instant Pot, for instance, has both an Egg setting and a Porridge setting.

Huevos Rancheros Casserole

Serves 4

PREP TIME: **10 MINUTES**

STEAM: **7 MINUTES HIGH PRESSURE**

RELEASE: **QUICK**

TOTAL TIME: **25 MINUTES**

Huevos rancheros is a great brunch dish, and it's easy to make for a crowd in the pressure cooker. There are many versions of it, but for the most part it's composed of lightly fried tortillas topped with beans, sauce, and fried eggs. Cooking everything together in the pressure cooker saves time and requires less cleanup. You can use canned black beans or cook your own black beans for this dish.

1. In the pressure-cooker pot, add 1 cup water and place the trivet inside.

2. Coat a 7-inch round baking dish with cooking spray and lay the tortillas on the bottom.

3. Pour the black beans on top of the tortillas. With a spoon, make four indentations in the beans, and then gently crack the eggs into the indentations. Season with salt and pepper.

4. Cover the dish with aluminum foil and carefully lower it onto the trivet. Close and lock the lid.

5. Select the Steam setting and cook for 7 minutes at high pressure. When cooking is complete, quick release the pressure. Carefully unlock and remove the lid.

6. Carefully remove the dish from the pressure cooker and remove the foil. Serve, topped with salsa roja, chopped cilantro, and queso fresco (if using).

Cooking spray

2 corn tortillas

1 (15-ounce) can black beans, drained or 1¾ cups cooked black beans

4 large eggs

Salt

Freshly ground black pepper

Salsa Roja (page 137) or store-bought salsa, for serving

Fresh cilantro leaves, chopped, for serving

Herby Queso Fresco (page 36), crema, or sour cream for serving (optional)

OPTION: Before serving, you can add some crema or sour cream, or sprinkle some store-bought or homemade queso fresco on top. If you don't have salsa roja, feel free to make a pico de gallo (diced tomatoes, onion, cilantro, lime juice, chile, salt, and pepper) or simply chop some fresh grape tomatoes and cilantro. You can also slice some avocado on the side, or make a quick guacamole. Either way, make sure you have some extra tortillas to pull together all the leftover goodness you'll have on your plate. I also like to finish this dish off with some flaky sea salt, for extra crunch and flavor.

Soft-Boiled Eggs with Kale and Salsa Verde

Serves 4

PREP TIME: **5 MINUTES**

MANUAL/PRESSURE COOK: **3 TO 5 MINUTES LOW PRESSURE**

RELEASE: **QUICK**

TOTAL TIME: **15 MINUTES**

4 large eggs

4 cups shredded kale

Juice of 1 lemon

Extra-virgin olive oil, for serving

Pinch flaky sea salt

Salsa Verde (page 138), for serving (optional)

The electric pressure cooker is great for cooking eggs. They keep well in the refrigerator for a couple of days, so I like to make six at a time and keep them handy for quick breakfasts or snacks.

OPTION: To elevate the dish, add some black sesame seeds and/or sunflower seeds, plus a bit of chopped cilantro or parsley.

1. In the pressure-cooker pot, add 1 cup water and place the trivet inside.

2. Arrange the eggs on the trivet. Close and lock the lid.

3. Select Manual/Pressure Cook and cook for 3 minutes at low pressure for a soft-boiled egg with a runny yolk, or 5 minutes at low pressure for a hard-boiled egg.

4. While the eggs are cooking, in a mixing bowl, toss the kale with the lemon juice, olive oil, and sea salt.

5. When cooking is complete, quick release the pressure. Unlock and carefully remove the lid. Rinse the eggs under cold water until cool, and peel. Cut the eggs in half.

6. On each plate, arrange the dressed kale, top with two halves of soft-boiled egg, and add the salsa verde (if using).

Shakshuka-Style Baked Eggs

Serves 6

PREP TIME: **10 MINUTES**

MANUAL/PRESSURE COOK: **2 TO 7 MINUTES LOW PRESSURE**

RELEASE: **QUICK**

TOTAL TIME: **25 MINUTES**

Shakshuka—eggs poached in a sauce of tomatoes and peppers—is a great dish for sharing. It's easy to make, even for a crowd, and full of flavor. The eggs cook right in the sauce, making it a one-pot meal. Serve it with warm pita-bread triangles for dipping and, ideally, some fried halloumi cheese on the side. Sumac is a Middle Eastern spice that adds a beautiful red color and an intense citrusy note to the dish.

1. In the pressure-cooker pot, add 1 cup of water and place the trivet inside.

2. In a 7-inch baking dish, add the sofrito sauce. With a wooden spoon, make six indentations in the sofrito. Crack each egg into one of the indentations, being careful not to break the yolks.

3. Season the eggs with salt and pepper. Cover the dish with aluminum foil and place it on the trivet. Close and lock the lid.

4. Select the Manual/Pressure Cook setting and cook for 7 minutes at low pressure for a set egg, or for a runnier yolk, cook for 2 minutes at low pressure. When cooking is complete, quick release the pressure. Unlock and carefully remove the lid.

5. Carefully remove the dish from the pressure cooker and remove the foil. Sprinkle the sumac and chopped cilantro on top, and serve.

2 cups Sofrito Base Sauce (page 140)

6 large eggs

Salt

Freshly ground black pepper

1 teaspoon sumac

Fresh cilantro leaves, chopped, for garnish

SUBSTITUTION: If you don't have sumac, substitute a bit of grated lemon peel, flaky sea salt, and pepper.

Spanish-Style Omelet (Tortilla Española)

Serves 6

PREP TIME: **10 MINUTES**

SAUTÉ: **15 MINUTES**

MANUAL/PRESSURE COOK: **15 MINUTES HIGH PRESSURE**

RELEASE: **NATURAL**

TOTAL TIME: **1 HOUR**

A Spanish-style omelet is similar to a frittata and is served cut into wedges. It's a fantastic make-ahead breakfast or an easy take-along picnic lunch, but I also like to serve it as an appetizer along with some manchego cheese, chorizo, and olives. The trick to making this dish successfully in an electric pressure cooker is to spray the baking dish very thoroughly with non-stick cooking spray so that the eggs don't stick.

1. Coat a 7-inch baking dish with cooking spray.

2. Select the Sauté setting and add the olive oil, onions, and potatoes. Add a bit of salt to help the onions release their moisture and start cooking. If they get too dry, add a bit more oil, until the potatoes are soft and the onions translucent. If they start getting brown, turn down the heat and cover them for a bit until they release more moisture. You don't want them to get brown or caramelized.

3. Keep stirring and moving the mixture with a wooden spoon so it doesn't stick to the bottom of the pan, for about 15 minutes, until tender. Once done, remove the potatoes and onions from the pot and set aside to cool.

4. Meanwhile, in a medium bowl, whisk the eggs.

5. Add the potato-and-onion mixture to the eggs, stir to combine, and pour into the prepared baking dish. Cover with aluminum foil.

Continued

Cooking spray

2 tablespoons extra-virgin olive oil

2 cups julienned onions

2 medium waxy potatoes (like red potatoes or fingerling potatoes), cut into thin rounds

8 large eggs

Salt

TECHNIQUE: Make sure the potatoes and onions are soft and seasoned well, because all that flavor will go into the omelet. If the potatoes still have a bit of a bite, they'll remain that way, so be sure to cook them through.

Spanish-Style Omelet (Tortilla Española) *Continued*

6. In the pressure-cooker pot, add 1½ cups water and place the trivet inside. Carefully lower the baking dish onto the trivet. Close and lock the lid.

7. Select the Manual/Pressure Cook setting and cook for 15 minutes at high pressure. When cooking is complete, allow the pressure to release naturally. Unlock and carefully remove the lid.

8. Carefully remove the dish from the pressure cooker. Remove the foil and unmold the frittata onto a plate. Serve.

Mini Mushroom and Cheese Quiches

Serves 4

PREP TIME: **10 MINUTES**

SAUTÉ: **5 MINUTES**

STEAM: **7 MINUTES HIGH PRESSURE**

RELEASE: **QUICK**

TOTAL TIME: **30 MINUTES**

I like to keep a stash of these adorable crustless mini quiches in my refrigerator at all times. They make a healthy and satisfying snack or a perfect on-the-go breakfast. They also make a nice lunch with a spinach salad on the side. This recipe is endlessly variable to suit your own taste; you can substitute other vegetables for the mushrooms and use any kind of cheese you desire.

1. Select the Sauté setting to preheat the pressure-cooker pot.

2. Add the olive oil and mushrooms. Season with salt, and cover for 2 minutes to release the moisture.

3. Uncover and continue sautéing for another 3 minutes, stirring regularly, until the mushrooms are cooked through.

4. Remove the mushrooms from the pot and set aside. Rinse and dry the pressure-cooker pot.

5. In a medium bowl, lightly beat the eggs. In the same bowl, add the mushrooms and cheese, and stir to combine. Season with salt and pepper.

Continued

2 tablespoons extra-virgin olive oil

3 cups sliced button mushrooms

Salt

8 large eggs

1 cup shredded Cheddar cheese

Freshly ground black pepper

Cooking spray

Fresh spinach, torn, for garnish

OPTION: You can do these with only egg whites for a healthier take. To save time and cleanup, use a 7-inch baking dish instead of individual ramekins.

Mini Mushroom and Cheese Quiches *Continued*

6. Spray four 6-ounce ramekins with cooking spray and pour ½ cup of the egg mixture into each ramekin. Cover each ramekin with aluminum foil.

7. In the pressure-cooker pot, add 1 cup of water and place the trivet inside. Carefully place the ramekins on the trivet. Close and lock the lid.

8. Select the Steam setting for 7 minutes at high pressure. When cooking is complete, quick release the pressure. Unlock and carefully remove the lid.

9. Carefully remove the ramekins from the cooker and remove the foil. Serve with spinach for garnish.

Breakfast Bowl with Poached Eggs, Avocado, and Salmon

Serves 4

PREP TIME: **10 MINUTES**

MANUAL/PRESSURE COOK: **1 MINUTE LOW PRESSURE**

RELEASE: **QUICK**

TOTAL TIME: **15 MINUTES**

Who doesn't love a poached egg, right? But cooking them usually requires so much stirring, watching, and babysitting that they often seem like too much trouble. Once you discover how easy it is to make perfect poached eggs in the electric pressure cooker, you'll never go back. Here I use those supercute silicone poach pods set on the trivet to cook the eggs. Sprinkle sesame seeds on top for an optional garnish.

1. In the pressure-cooker pot, add 1 cup water and place the trivet inside.

2. Crack one egg in each poach pod and season with salt. Carefully place the poach pods on the trivet. Close and lock the lid.

3. Select the Manual/Pressure Cook setting and cook the eggs for 1 minute on low pressure.

4. While the eggs cook, halve, pit, and peel the avocado, and slice it into thin wedges. Dress with some of the lemon juice, and season with salt and pepper to taste.

5. When cooking is complete, quick release the pressure. Unlock and carefully remove the lid. Remove the eggs from the cooking pot and set aside.

6. Divide the watercress among four bowls and dress with a bit of lemon juice, olive oil, and flaky sea salt. Slide an egg into the middle of each bowl and place the salmon and avocado slices on the side. Garnish with sesame seeds (if using) and serve.

4 large eggs

Salt

1 avocado

Juice of 1 lemon

Freshly ground black pepper

6 ounces watercress

8 ounces smoked salmon, sliced

Extra-virgin olive oil

Flaky sea salt

Sesame seeds for garnish (optional)

OPTION: You can do any flavor combination you like in this bowl. Substitute arugula for the watercress, add quinoa to make it more filling, or swap out the salmon for any other white smoked fish you like.

Morocho Buckwheat Porridge

Serves 4 to 6

PREP TIME: **5 MINUTES**
PORRIDGE: **7 MINUTES**
RELEASE: **QUICK**
TOTAL TIME: **20 MINUTES**

This is a take on a classic Ecuadorian drink called *morocho*, but I use buckwheat instead of corn. The buckwheat gives it a thicker consistency, making it more of a hot cereal than a beverage. The condensed milk is optional, but a little bit of this thick, sweet, creamy topping goes a long way, and kids especially will love it. Buckwheat is naturally gluten-free and high in protein, making this a nutritious and satisfying breakfast.

1. In the pressure-cooker pot, add 1 cup water and place the trivet inside.

2. In a 7-inch baking dish, combine the buckwheat, whole milk, condensed milk (if using), cinnamon sticks, and cloves. Cover with aluminum foil and place on the trivet. Close and lock the lid.

3. Select the Porridge setting and cook for 7 minutes. When cooking is complete, quick release the pressure. Unlock and carefully remove the lid.

4. Carefully remove the baking dish from the cooker. When cool enough to handle, remove the foil, cinnamon sticks, and cloves. Mix well and enjoy topped with dried fruit, toasted coconut flakes, or cocoa nibs (if using).

1 cup cream of buckwheat

4 cups whole milk

½ cup sweetened condensed milk (optional)

2 whole cinnamon sticks

6 whole cloves

¼ cup chopped dried fruit, toasted coconut flakes, or cocoa nibs (optional)

TROUBLESHOOTING: Don't skip the insert for this one! I've made this several times directly in the pressure cooker and it always burned, so be sure to use the baking dish and cover with foil.

Butternut Squash and Coconut Porridge

Serves 4 to 6

PREP TIME: **5 MINUTES**

MANUAL/PRESSURE COOK: **6 MINUTES HIGH PRESSURE**

RELEASE: **QUICK OR NATURAL**

TOTAL TIME: **20 MINUTES**

This simple porridge is an easy and nutritious breakfast for the whole family. Butternut squash is more commonly used in savory soups, but it makes a great cold-day breakfast, too. The sweetness of the squash pairs beautifully with creamy coconut milk and warming spices. I like to sprinkle pumpkin seeds, blueberries, or chopped banana over the top and add a drizzle of maple syrup.

1. In the pressure-cooker pot, add the butternut squash, coconut milk, ginger, nutmeg, and cinnamon stick, along with ¼ cup water. Close and lock the lid.

2. Select the Manual/Pressure Cook setting and cook for 6 minutes at high pressure. When cooking is complete, quick release the pressure or allow it to release naturally. Carefully unlock and remove the lid.

3. Using a slotted spoon, remove the butternut squash chunks and transfer to a mixing bowl. Mash with a fork or immersion blender and add the cooking liquid little by little until your desired consistency is achieved.

4. If desired, finish the dish as follows: sprinkle with pumpkin seeds, add a splash of maple syrup, or top with some bananas or berries, and/or almond butter or peanut butter.

4 cups cubed butternut squash

1 (13.5-ounce) can coconut milk

1 teaspoon grated fresh ginger or ¼ teaspoon ground ginger

¼ teaspoon ground nutmeg

1 cinnamon stick or ¼ teaspoon ground cinnamon

Pumpkin seeds (optional)

Maple syrup (optional)

Banana, chopped (optional)

Blueberries (optional)

Peanut butter or almond butter (optional)

TECHNIQUE: I highly recommend using the slotted spoon to take the squash out of the pot and then add the liquid. Don't just blend everything at the same time—there will be too much liquid. Consistency is key in this dish, and you want it to be a porridge, not a soup.

Bircher Muesli

Makes 2 cups

PREP TIME: **5 MINUTES**

MANUAL/PRESSURE COOK: **2 MINUTES HIGH PRESSURE**

RELEASE: **QUICK**

TOTAL TIME: **20 MINUTES**

I discovered Bircher muesli when I was in London and fell in love with it. I ate it nearly every day for breakfast. It's traditionally made by soaking oats in apple juice overnight, but you can make it in just a few minutes in the electric pressure cooker. You still get all the lovely flavor and sweetness from the apple juice, but in a fraction of the time.

1. In the pressure-cooker pot, add 1 cup water and place the trivet inside.

2. In a 7-inch baking dish, combine the oats and apple juice. Cover with foil. Place the baking dish on the trivet. Close and lock the lid.

3. Use the Manual/Pressure Cook setting and cook for 2 minutes at high pressure. When cooking is complete, quick release the pressure. Unlock and carefully remove the lid.

4. Carefully remove the baking dish. Let stand for about 10 minutes to cool. Remove the foil.

5. To serve, fold in yogurt and/or milk to achieve desired consistency. Top with dried fruit.

1 cup old-fashioned rolled oats

2 cups apple juice

Yogurt or milk, for serving

Dried fruit, such as raisins or apricots, for serving

OPTION: If you'd like to add dried fruit to the muesli during the cooking process, add it in with the oats and juice in step 2. The dried fruit will rehydrate during the cooking process.

Sausage and Cheese Frittata

Serves 4

PREP TIME: **10 MINUTES**

MANUAL/PRESSURE COOK: **15 MINUTES HIGH PRESSURE**

RELEASE: **QUICK**

TOTAL TIME: **40 MINUTES**

You can't help but love this decadent breakfast or brunch frittata that's loaded with cheese and your favorite sausage. Plus, it's so easy to make in the electric pressure cooker that you'll never want to make individual omelets for your family and friends again.

1. In the pressure-cooker pot, add 1 cup of water and place the trivet inside.

2. Cut a parchment round and place it in the bottom of a 7-inch baking dish. Use the butter to coat the sides of the dish and the top of the parchment.

3. In a medium bowl, whisk the eggs, milk, salt, pepper, and nutmeg (if using) very well. Add the sausage, Cheddar cheese, and herbs, and whisk until combined.

4. Pour the mixture into the prepared baking dish. Cover loosely with foil, and place inside the pressure-cooker pot. Close and lock the lid in place.

5. Select Manual/Pressure Cook and cook on high pressure for 15 minutes. When cooking is complete, quick release the pressure. Unlock and carefully remove the lid.

6. Carefully remove the baking dish and let rest for about 5 minutes. When cool enough to handle, remove the foil, place a large plate over the baking dish, and invert onto a serving plate. Serve immediately.

1 tablespoon butter

6 large eggs

½ cup whole milk

Salt

Freshly ground black pepper

⅛ teaspoon ground nutmeg (optional)

2 cups ½-inch slices of ready-to-eat breakfast-sausage links

1 cup shredded sharp Cheddar cheese

2 tablespoons chopped fresh parsley, scallions, tarragon, and/or chives

INGREDIENT TIP: Be adventurous with the fresh herbs in this dish, as they can add so much flavor to the simple ingredients. Tarragon, dill, and chives all work well, but feel free to be creative and make the dish unique to your tastes.

Herby Queso Fresco

Makes 1½ cups

PREP TIME: **3 MINUTES**

YOGURT SETTING: **30 MINUTES**

TOTAL TIME: **45 MINUTES, PLUS OVERNIGHT RESTING**

Even homemade cheese is easy to make in your electric pressure cooker! This fresh cheese gets its bright, herby flavor from the handful of cilantro that's stirred in at the end, but you could substitute another herb if you prefer. It keeps well in the refrigerator for several days. I love to smear it on a toasted slice of cassava bread and top it with avocado slices. It's one of my favorite breakfasts.

1. In the pressure-cooker pot, add the milk. Close and lock the lid, leaving the steam vent open.

2. Select the Yogurt setting on boil for 30 minutes.

3. When complete, turn the pressure cooker off, remove the lid, and carefully take out the cooking pot. Set it on a heatproof surface and stir in the vinegar. Let sit for about 3 minutes, until curds begin to form.

4. Once the curds have set, stir in the salt.

5. Line a colander with cheesecloth, and pour the mixture into it. Drain until the curds look drier, about 5 minutes. Stir in the chopped cilantro and mix well.

6. Transfer the cheesecloth with the curds into a small dish. Fold the sides of the cheesecloth over the curds, and cover with plastic wrap. Top with a plate and then set a weight (a jar of sauce or a can of beans) on top of the plate. Refrigerate overnight; the cheese will become firm.

7. Remove the cheesecloth and transfer the cheese to an airtight container. It keeps for up to 3 days in the refrigerator.

8 cups whole milk

¼ cup white vinegar

1 tablespoon salt

¼ cup chopped fresh cilantro

INGREDIENT TIP: Fold in whatever herbs you like, or divide the mixture and fold cilantro and flaky sea salt into one and oregano and parsley into the other. You'll have two cheeses with very different flavor profiles.

Challah Bread Pudding

Serves 4 to 6

PREP TIME: **10 MINUTES**
MANUAL/PRESSURE COOK: **20 MINUTES LOW PRESSURE**
RELEASE: **NATURAL FOR 10 MINUTES, THEN QUICK**
TOTAL TIME: **50 MINUTES**

The electric pressure cooker has changed the way I feel about making brunch for a large group, because it makes it so easy to whip up a big pot of delicious food with very little effort. This dish is a cross between bread pudding and French toast. It's comfort food at its best, so be prepared to become instantly addicted. I recommend using fresh challah, but you can use any bread, even if it's a bit stale. If you're using stale bread, increase the milk by ¼ cup to make sure it doesn't turn out too dry.

1. In the pressure-cooker pot, add 1 cup water and place the trivet inside.

2. Use the butter to coat the bottom and sides of a 7-inch baking dish. Fill the dish with the bread cubes.

3. In a small bowl, whisk the eggs, milk, syrup, vanilla, cinnamon, and nutmeg until just combined. Season with salt.

4. Pour the egg mixture over the bread and let sit until the bread is fully soaked, about 5 minutes. Cover with aluminum foil and lower the pan onto the trivet. Close and lock the lid.

5. Select the Manual/Pressure Cook setting and cook for 20 minutes at low pressure. When cooking is complete, allow the pressure to naturally release for 10 minutes, then quick release any remaining pressure.

6. Carefully unlock and remove the lid. Carefully remove the baking dish and foil. Serve warm.

1 tablespoon butter

8 slices challah bread, cut into 1-inch cubes

3 large eggs

1 cup whole milk

⅓ cup pure maple syrup

2 teaspoons pure vanilla extract

1 tablespoon ground cinnamon (optional)

¼ teaspoon ground nutmeg (optional)

Pinch salt

OPTION: If you want a little extra sweetness, serve with Homemade Mixed Berry Sauce (page 144) or Apple Compote (page 145), or simply sprinkle powdered sugar on top.

**Farro, Radish, Fennel, and Red Onion
Salad with Herbed Yogurt Dressing,** *page 50*

CHAPTER 4
Sides & Starters

I love using my electric pressure cooker to cook all kinds of sides, from vegetables to grains, because it's so effortless. I can just set up the cooker, turn it on, and then focus on the rest of the meal, knowing that whatever is in the pressure cooker will turn out perfectly.

The Instant Pot includes settings for Rice, Multigrain, and Bean/Chili, while the Power Pressure Cooker XL has Fish/Vegetables Steam, Beans/Lentils, and Rice/Risotto. Cosori's version includes Beans/Chili, White Rice, Brown Rice, Multigrain, Steam Vegetables, and Steam Potatoes.

Quinoa Medley with Tomatoes

Serves 4 to 6

PREP TIME: **10 MINUTES**

SAUTÉ: **1 MINUTE**

MANUAL/PRESSURE COOK: **1 MINUTE HIGH PRESSURE**

RELEASE: **NATURAL FOR 10 MINUTES, THEN QUICK**

TOTAL TIME: **40 MINUTES**

Quinoa is full of protein and fiber, making it a healthy choice as a side dish. It also has a mild taste, which makes it a great backdrop for the fresh flavors of peppers and tomatoes. This dish is delicious as a side, or it can be used as the base for a grain salad. If you like a spicy kick, substitute jalapeño pepper for some or all of the bell pepper.

1. Select the Sauté setting to preheat the pressure-cooker pot, and set to high heat. Add the olive oil, bell peppers, celery, salt, and pepper. Cook for 1 minute, then add the quinoa and stock. Stir to combine. Close and lock the lid.

2. Use the Manual/Pressure Cook setting and cook for 1 minute at high pressure. When cooking is complete, allow the pressure to release naturally for 10 minutes, then quick release any remaining pressure. Unlock and carefully remove the lid.

3. Fold in the tomatoes and basil or oregano. Season with additional salt and pepper. Serve immediately, at room temperature or cold.

1 tablespoon extra-virgin olive oil

2 medium bell peppers, finely diced

4 celery stalks, finely diced

1 teaspoon salt, plus more for seasoning

½ teaspoon freshly ground black pepper, plus more for seasoning

1 cup red or mixed quinoa

1⅔ cups Chicken Stock (page 134), beef stock (see Shredded Beef, page 96), Vegetable Stock (page 136), or water

1 pint cherry or grape tomatoes, halved

1 tablespoon chopped fresh basil or oregano

OPTION: If I'm having people over, I like to buy whole heirloom tomatoes, remove the insides, and stuff them with this quinoa mix. I serve them on a platter of dressed arugula or watercress for a pretty and filling dish.

Yuca with Cuban Mojo Sauce

Serves 4

PREP TIME: **5 MINUTES**

MANUAL/PRESSURE COOK: **8 MINUTES HIGH PRESSURE**

RELEASE: **NATURAL**

TOTAL TIME: **30 MINUTES**

Yuca (also known as cassava or tapioca) is a starchy root vegetable common in Latin American cuisine. It's similar to a white potato, but higher in fiber. Throughout Latin America, it's eaten the way we eat potatoes in the United States. Like potato, yuca is mildly flavored, so it serves as a nice starchy backdrop for whatever seasonings you add.

1. In the pressure-cooker pot, add 1 cup of water and place the trivet inside.

2. Arrange the yuca pieces on the trivet. Close and lock the lid.

3. Select the Manual/Pressure Cook setting and cook for 8 minutes at high pressure. When cooking is complete, allow the pressure to release naturally. Unlock and carefully remove the lid.

4. Arrange the yuca in a bowl and season with salt. Drizzle the mojo sauce on the yuca and serve.

½ pound frozen peeled yuca root pieces

Salt

¼ cup Cuban Mojo Sauce (page 143)

TECHNIQUE: Pour the mojo on top of the yuca while it's still hot. As with potatoes, yuca absorbs flavorful sauces better when it is hot.

Sweet Potato Gratin

Serves 4

PREP TIME: **20 MINUTES**

MANUAL/PRESSURE COOK: **25 MINUTES HIGH PRESSURE**

RELEASE: **NATURAL**

TOTAL TIME: **1 HOUR**

Sweet potatoes are a great change from regular white potatoes. They're more nutritious and, to me at least, more delicious. They have tons of flavor and are also full of nutrients. I used to roast them to a golden brown in the oven, but this pressure-cooker recipe has become one of my favorites. The sweet potatoes are cooked in cream and topped with grated Parmesan and fresh thyme leaves, making for an easy side dish that is luxurious to eat.

1. In the pressure-cooker pot, add 1 cup of water and place the trivet inside.

2. Lightly coat the inside of a 7-inch baking dish or springform pan with cooking spray.

3. Using a mandoline or sharp knife, slice the sweet potatoes crosswise into ⅛-inch slices.

4. In the baking dish, make a layer of sweet potato slices, overlapping each slice by about ½ inch.

5. With a tablespoon measure, drizzle about 3 tablespoons of heavy cream over the first layer. Sprinkle with 2 pinches of salt and 1 pinch of black pepper.

Cooking spray

2 medium sweet
   potatoes, peeled

1 cup plus 2 tablespoons
   heavy cream

Salt

Freshly ground black pepper

1 cup plus 2 tablespoons
   grated Parmesan cheese

3 tablespoons fresh
   thyme leaves

TECHNIQUE: Build this dish just like you'd build a lasagna. If you want to get the Parmesan golden brown on top, put the finished dish in the oven on the broil setting for a few minutes.

6. Sprinkle a scant 3 tablespoons of grated Parmesan cheese and a big pinch of thyme leaves on top.

7. Make a second layer of sweet potato slices, heavy cream, salt, pepper, grated Parmesan, and thyme.

8. Continue making layers until you run out of sweet potato. You will have about 6 layers in total, ending with grated Parmesan and thyme on top.

9. Cover the baking dish with foil and carefully lower it into the pressure-cooker pot. Close and lock the lid.

10. Select the Manual/Pressure Cook setting and cook for 25 minutes at high pressure. When cooking is complete, allow the pressure to naturally release. Unlock and carefully remove the lid.

11. Carefully remove the baking dish and take off the foil. Serve directly from the baking dish, or pop it out of the dish after letting rest for about 5 minutes.

Pesto Rice

Serves 4

PREP TIME: **5 MINUTES**

RICE OR MANUAL/PRESSURE COOK: **8 MINUTES HIGH PRESSURE**

RELEASE: **QUICK**

TOTAL TIME: **30 MINUTES**

1 cup jasmine rice

1 teaspoon salt, plus more for seasoning

1 tablespoon canola oil or other neutral-flavored oil

¼ cup Pesto Sauce (page 142) or your favorite store-bought pesto

I grew up eating rice nearly every day; even when we had pasta, there was always rice, too, just in case someone wanted it. My grandmother was always trying to find creative ways to serve it. I learned from her that stirring in a dollop of pesto gives this humble grain tons of flavor and makes it much more special than just plain rice. Serve this dish alongside chicken, fish, or roasted meats to fancy up a simple family meal.

TECHNIQUE: In this recipe, I let the rice cool and then fold in the pesto. If you add the pesto when the rice is too hot, you lose the bright green color of the herbs. You can let the rice cool naturally, or, if you're in a hurry and want it done in less than 30 minutes, put the rice in a container and place it in the fridge until cool before stirring in the pesto.

1. In the pressure-cooker pot, add the rice, 1 cup water, and the salt. Close and lock the lid.

2. Select the Rice or Manual/Pressure Cook setting and cook for 8 minutes at high pressure. When cooking is complete, quick release the pressure. Unlock and carefully remove the lid.

3. Use a fork to fluff the rice, and let cool. When cool, fold in the pesto with a spatula, and season with salt. Serve immediately.

Polenta

Serves 4 to 6

PREP TIME: **3 MINUTES**

MANUAL/PRESSURE COOK: **10 MINUTES HIGH PRESSURE**

RELEASE: **NATURAL**

TOTAL TIME: **30 MINUTES**

Polenta is a simple dish, a cooked cornmeal porridge that, while easy to make, normally requires quite a bit of stirring and babysitting. But the electric pressure cooker makes preparing it a breeze. It's okay if the polenta is a bit loose when it's finished cooking; it will thicken as it cools. Feel free to stir in your choice of herbs such as chives, dill, or tarragon along with the cheese and parsley.

1. In the pressure-cooker pot, add 1 cup of water and place the trivet inside.

2. In a 7-inch baking dish, add the polenta, salt, olive oil, and 4 cups water. Cover the dish with aluminum foil and carefully lower it into the pressure-cooker pot. Close and lock the lid.

3. Select the Manual/Pressure Cook setting and cook for 10 minutes at high pressure. When cooking is complete, allow the pressure to release naturally. Unlock and carefully remove the lid.

4. Carefully remove the baking dish and foil, whisk in the grated Parmesan cheese and parsley, and season with more salt. Serve immediately.

1 cup polenta

1 teaspoon salt, plus more for seasoning

3 tablespoons extra-virgin olive oil

½ cup grated Parmesan cheese

½ cup chopped fresh parsley

MAKE-AHEAD TIP: Polenta keeps great in the fridge for up to 3 days. It will firm up a bit, so when you want to reheat it, add a bit of milk to loosen it up.

Mexican-Style Corn

Serves 4

PREP TIME: **5 MINUTES**

STEAM: **2 MINUTES**

SAUTÉ: **5 MINUTES ON HIGH**

RELEASE: **QUICK**

TOTAL TIME: **15 MINUTES**

In Mexico, you'll see street carts selling versions of this savory corn-on-the-cob snack everywhere, and it's a favorite in my family. I usually make it on the barbecue, but this pressure-cooker version is great because it's quick and easy to cook, yet still has all those authentic Mexican flavors from the Herby Queso Fresco (page 36), chili flakes, lime, and cilantro. It makes a festive side dish or satisfying afternoon snack.

1. In the pressure-cooker pot, add 1 cup water and place the trivet inside.

2. Place the corn halves on the trivet, and close and lock the lid.

3. Select the Steam setting and cook for 2 minutes. When cooking is complete, quick release the pressure. Unlock and carefully remove the lid.

4. Remove the trivet and discard the water from the pressure-cooker pot. Wipe the pot dry and return it to the cooker.

5. Switch the pressure cooker to the Sauté function on high, and cook the corn with the butter and oil for about 5 minutes, until it has some golden-brown spots throughout.

6. Remove the corn pieces from the pot and serve, garnished with queso fresco, red pepper flakes, lime wedges (if using), and cilantro (if using).

2 ears of corn, shucked and halved

2 tablespoons butter

1 tablespoon canola oil or other neutral-flavored oil

Herby Queso Fresco (page 36), for garnish

Red pepper flakes (use regular or guajillo chili flakes), for garnish

Lime wedges, for garnish (optional)

Fresh cilantro leaves, chopped, for garnish (optional)

TECHNIQUE: To get some nice golden-brown caramelization on the corn, make sure the oil and butter are hot before putting the corn in. The reason I use a butter-and-oil combo is that if you only use butter, it burns too quickly and gets black before the corn gets caramelized. If you're doing a large batch, it's better to steam the corn in the pressure cooker and then either caramelize it in a cast-iron pan on the stove top or brush it with oil and butter and caramelize it in the oven.

Chinese-Style Bok Choy with Shiitake Mushrooms

Serves 4

PREP TIME: **5 MINUTES**

SAUTÉ: **5 MINUTES**

STEAM: **1 MINUTE HIGH PRESSURE**

RELEASE: **QUICK**

TOTAL TIME: **15 MINUTES**

Bok choy, also called Chinese cabbage, is a leafy dark-green vegetable. For a leafy green, it's uniquely juicy and flavorful, and I find it a welcome change from broccoli. I like to use baby bok choy because it's easy to handle—plus it's just adorable! In this recipe, it's cooked with shiitake mushrooms and sweet-savory oyster sauce to create a simple but satisfying side dish.

1. Select the Sauté setting and add the olive oil and mushrooms to the pressure-cooker pot. Season with salt. Sauté for about 5 minutes, until the mushrooms are lightly browned, then remove them from the pot and set aside.

2. In the pressure-cooker pot, add the bok choy, sesame oil, oyster sauce, soy sauce, and ¼ cup water. Close and lock the lid.

3. Select the Steam setting and cook for 1 minute at high pressure. When cooking is complete, quick release the pressure. Unlock and carefully remove the lid.

4. Transfer the bok choy to a serving plate, and top with the reserved mushrooms.

1 tablespoon extra-virgin olive oil

2 cups sliced shiitake mushrooms

Salt

2 baby bok choy heads, quartered lengthwise

2 tablespoons sesame oil

2 tablespoons oyster sauce

1 teaspoon soy sauce

SUBSTITUTION: To save a little time, you can also serve the bok choy with chopped raw button mushrooms on top instead of the cooked shiitake.

Green Beans with Capers and Bell Pepper

Serves 4 to 6

PREP TIME: **5 MINUTES**

STEAM: **1 MINUTE**

SAUTÉ: **1 MINUTE**

RELEASE: **QUICK**

TOTAL TIME: **15 MINUTES**

1 tablespoon extra-virgin
  olive oil

1 pound green
  beans, trimmed

1 red bell pepper, julienned

1 teaspoon ground cumin

1 scallion, thinly sliced

3 tablespoons
  capers, drained

Salt

Freshly ground black pepper

I love green beans cooked to a perfect crisp-tender texture, which you can get with only 1 minute of cooking in the pressure cooker. They're great with just a splash of lemon juice, a drizzle of olive oil, and a sprinkling of flaky sea salt, but I love to dress them up with capers and bell pepper, too. The inspiration for this dish came from the Jewish deli on the corner.

OPTION: If you're pressed for time, another option is to just steam the green beans, then add the sliced bell pepper and capers raw, and combine with the rest of the ingredients.

1. In the pressure-cooker pot, add 1 cup of water and place the trivet inside.

2. Arrange the green beans in a steamer basket and lower it into the pot. Close and lock the lid.

3. Select the Steam setting and cook for 1 minute. When cooking is complete, quick release the pressure. Unlock and carefully open the lid.

4. Remove the steamer basket and trivet, and discard the water. Wipe the pressure-cooker pot dry and return it to the cooker.

5. Use the Sauté function to heat the pressure-cooker pot. When hot, add the olive oil, green beans, and red pepper. Sauté about 1 minute, until light golden brown. Add the cumin, scallion, and capers, and stir until just combined. Watch out—the capers might pop as they release their moisture.

6. Season with salt and pepper, and serve.

Wild Rice Pilaf

Serves 4

PREP TIME: **5 MINUTES**

MANUAL/PRESSURE COOK: **18 MINUTES HIGH PRESSURE**

RELEASE: **NATURAL**

TOTAL TIME: **50 MINUTES**

Wild rice is gorgeous to look at with its varying colors and textures, but it normally takes a long time to cook, so it often ends up relegated to special occasions. The electric pressure cooker cooks it in a fraction of the time, making it suitable for any day of the week. Add tart sweet dried cranberries, crunchy almonds, and fresh mint, and you have a party! Serve it alongside your favorite protein.

1. In the pressure-cooker pot, add the rice and 4 cups water. Season with salt. Close and lock the lid.

2. Select the Manual/Pressure Cook setting and cook for 18 minutes at high pressure. When cooking is complete, allow the pressure to release naturally. Unlock and carefully remove the lid. Drain any remaining water.

3. Allow the rice to cool, then fold in the cranberries, almonds, mint, olive oil, lime juice, and lime zest. Season with salt, and serve.

2 cups wild rice

Salt

½ cup dried cranberries

⅓ cup almonds, sliced or slivered

½ cup chopped fresh mint

1 tablespoon extra-virgin olive oil

Juice of 1 lime

Zest of ¼ lime

SUBSTITUTION: For an alternate version you can swap in pomegranate seeds for the cranberries, chopped pistachios for the almonds, and/or parsley for the mint.

Farro, Radish, Fennel, and Red Onion Salad with Herbed Yogurt Dressing

Serves 4 to 6

PREP TIME: **15 MINUTES**

SAUTÉ: **2 MINUTES**

MANUAL/PRESSURE COOK: **8 MINUTES HIGH PRESSURE**

RELEASE: **QUICK**

TOTAL TIME: **30 MINUTES**

Farro, an ancient type of wheat that's full of nutrients, is super trendy lately, showing up on both restaurant menus and supermarket shelves. Like barley, farro has a toothsome bite when cooked. I love it tossed with crisp fresh veggies, as in this salad. A tangy, creamy yogurt-based dressing ties it all together. I could eat this salad for lunch every day.

1. Select the Sauté setting to preheat the pressure-cooker pot.

2. When hot, add the olive oil, farro, and salt. Brown for about 2 minutes, until the farro smells a bit nutty. Pour in 1 cup water and stir. Close and lock the lid.

3. Select the Manual/Pressure Cook setting and cook for 8 minutes at high pressure. When cooking is complete, quick release the pressure. Unlock and carefully open the lid. Drain the farro.

4. In a mixing bowl, toss the farro, radishes, fennel, and onion. Drizzle with the yogurt-herb dressing, adding a little at a time until the desired constancy is achieved. Top with chopped pistachios, if desired. Serve.

1 tablespoon extra-virgin olive oil

1 cup farro

1 teaspoon salt

3 or 4 radishes, sliced

¼ fennel bulb, thinly sliced

¼ red onion, sliced

½ cup store-bought yogurt-herb dressing

Chopped pistachios (optional)

OPTION: This salad also works great with leftover quinoa or wild rice in place of farro.

Potatoes with Chimichurri

Serves 4 to 6

PREP TIME: **5 MINUTES**

STEAM: **2 MINUTES**

SAUTÉ: **4 MINUTES**

RELEASE: **QUICK**

TOTAL TIME: **15 MINUTES**

Chimichurri (page 141) is a staple in Argentina and in Uruguay, where my mother lives. It has a permanent spot on the table and gets added to everything—bread, meat, chicken, fish, and, of course, potatoes. Potatoes take on a ton of personality when you top them with this very simple yet very flavorful herby "dressing." I use little creamer potatoes here, because I love their texture, they absorb the sauce well, and they're just so cute.

1. In the pressure-cooker pot, add 1 cup of water and place the trivet inside.

2. Halve the creamer potatoes and arrange them in a steamer basket. Lower the steamer basket into the pressure-cooker pot. Close and lock the lid.

3. Select the Steam setting and cook for 2 minutes. When cooking is complete, quick release the pressure. Unlock and carefully remove the lid. If the potatoes aren't tender enough when pierced with a fork, replace and lock the lid and steam for 1 more minute.

4. Remove the steamer basket and discard the water from the pressure-cooker pot. Wipe the pot dry and return it to the cooker.

Continued

1½ pounds creamer potatoes (each potato about 1 inch in diameter)

5 tablespoons Chimichurri (page 141), divided

Salt

Freshly ground black pepper

OPTION: If your potatoes are bigger, or if you'd like to keep them whole, add 1 more minute on the Steam setting in step 2. Potatoes absorb sauce better when they're hot, so add as much chimichurri as you like—but remember that a little goes a long way.

Potatoes with Chimichurri *Continued*

5. Heat the pressure-cooker pot using the Sauté setting. Add 2 tablespoons of chimichurri and half of the potatoes, cut-side down. Season with salt and pepper. Sear for about 2 minutes, without turning the potatoes, until they're golden brown and crispy. Stir well and transfer the first batch of potatoes to a plate.

6. Add 2 more tablespoons of chimichurri and the remaining potatoes, cut-side down. Season with salt and pepper, sear, and transfer to the same plate.

7. Add the remaining 1 tablespoon of chimichurri to the finished potatoes. Serve immediately or at room temperature.

Honey-Glazed Carrots

Serves 4

PREP TIME: **5 MINUTES**

STEAM: **1 MINUTE**

SAUTÉ: **1 MINUTE**

RELEASE: **QUICK**

TOTAL TIME: **15 MINUTES**

Naturally sweet carrots glazed with orange juice and honey make a great accompaniment to any kind of protein—especially lamb. To take this recipe up a notch, top it with diced fresh figs when they're in season.

1. In the pressure-cooker pot, add 1 cup of water and place the trivet inside.

2. Cut the carrots in half crosswise, and then in half lengthwise, if needed, so that all the pieces are roughly the same size, about 1 inch in diameter. Arrange the carrots in a steamer basket and lower the basket into the pressure-cooker pot. Close and lock the lid.

3. Select the Steam setting and cook for 1 minute for crisp-tender carrots or 2 minutes for more tender carrots. When cooking is complete, quick release the pressure. Unlock and carefully remove the lid.

4. Remove the steamer basket and trivet, and discard the water. Wipe the pressure-cooker pot clean and return it to the cooker.

5. Select the Sauté setting. In the pressure-cooker pot, combine the orange juice, honey, ginger, and paprika. Sauté the glaze about 1 minute, until it starts to thicken and bubble.

6. Add the carrots and stir until well coated in the glaze. Season with salt and pepper.

7. Serve at once, topped with black sesame seeds and/or chopped cilantro or chives (if using).

1 pound medium
    carrots, peeled

½ cup orange juice

2 tablespoons honey

½ teaspoon grated
    fresh ginger

½ teaspoon ground paprika

Salt

Freshly ground black pepper

Black sesame seeds
    (optional)

Fresh cilantro leaves or
    chives, chopped (optional)

OPTION: You can also add some sliced, toasted almonds as a garnish. For a more refined presentation, cut the carrots in faux tournée—a shape resembling a football.

Cauliflower Steaks with Mustard Mojo

Serves 4

PREP TIME: **5 MINUTES**

SAUTÉ: **15 MINUTES**

MANUAL/PRESSURE COOK: **2 MINUTES HIGH PRESSURE**

RELEASE: **QUICK**

TOTAL TIME: **30 MINUTES**

Cauliflower develops a rich sweetness when it's caramelized in a hot pan. I love to slice it into thick "steaks," brown them in the pot, and then finish cooking them under pressure with a tangy mustard mojo sauce. These steaks make a fun vegetarian entrée or a hearty side dish.

1. Cut the cauliflower in half and then cut the "steaks" from the middle out, about 1 inch thick.

2. Select the Sauté setting to preheat the pressure-cooker pot.

3. When the pressure-cooker pot is hot, add the oil and place the steaks in the pot to brown in batches, for about 5 minutes per batch, until they're browned in spots all over.

4. Return all the cauliflower to the pot, and add the garlic, mustard, and ¼ cup water. Close and lock the lid.

5. Select the Manual/Pressure Cook setting and cook for 2 minutes at high pressure. When cooking is complete, quick release the pressure. Unlock and carefully remove the lid.

6. Remove the cauliflower and transfer to a serving plate. Spoon the sauce over the cauliflower, and finish with the parsley and a squeeze of lemon juice. Season with salt and pepper.

1 whole cauliflower head

2 tablespoons extra-virgin olive oil

2 garlic cloves, minced

4 tablespoons Dijon mustard

¼ cup chopped fresh parsley

Squeeze of lemon juice

Salt

Freshly ground black pepper

OPTION: To get a good "steak," make sure you buy a large cauliflower and cut from the middle out with a very sharp knife. If not, it will fall apart. Alternatively, you can just cut it into florets, steam it, and add the mojo on top. Mojo also goes well with broccoli.

Plantains with Cheese

Serves 4

PREP TIME: **5 MINUTES**

STEAM: **5 MINUTES HIGH PRESSURE**

RELEASE: **QUICK**

TOTAL TIME: **15 MINUTES**

- -

I grew up eating plantains every day. We would slice them and fry them as *tajadas*, mash them like potatoes, steam them, boil them, or bake them whole in the oven. The variations were endless, but my favorite way to eat plantains is steamed with a bit of butter and some queso fresco or mozzarella on top. This is a healthy, simple, and delicious side dish that goes with almost everything.

1. Keeping the skin on, cut the ends off the plantains and cut each plantain in half.

2. In the pressure-cooker pot, add 1 cup water and place a steamer basket inside. Put the plantains in the basket. Close and lock the lid.

3. Select the Steam setting and cook for 5 minutes at high pressure. When cooking is complete, quick release the pressure. Unlock and carefully remove the lid.

4. Carefully remove the plantains and cut in half lengthwise. Add the butter and cheese, and serve.

2 very ripe plantains

1 tablespoon butter

½ cup Herby Queso Fresco (page 36) or shredded mozzarella cheese

- - - - - - - - - - - - - - -

OPTION: If desired, you can remove the skin after cooking, or keep it on to serve.

Brussels Sprouts with Kale and Sumac

Serves 4 to 6

PREP TIME: **5 MINUTES**

STEAM: **2 MINUTES HIGH PRESSURE**

SAUTÉ: **3 MINUTES**

RELEASE: **QUICK**

TOTAL TIME: **15 MINUTES**

I used to dress up vegetables with lemon juice. Then I discovered sumac, a Middle Eastern spice with an intense, citrusy flavor, and now that's what I sprinkle over all my veggies. I especially love to add it to dark-green, leafy vegetables, like Brussels sprouts and kale, because it balances out any bitterness. Because I leave the Brussels sprouts whole in this dish, it's one of the easiest Brussels sprouts recipes around.

1. In the pressure-cooker pot, add 1 cup water and place the trivet inside.

2. Arrange the Brussels sprouts in a steamer basket and lower it into the pressure-cooker pot. Close and lock the lid.

3. Select the Steam setting and cook for 2 minutes at high pressure. When cooking is complete, quick release the pressure. Unlock and carefully open the lid. If the sprouts aren't tender enough when pierced with a fork, replace and lock the lid and steam for 1 more minute.

1 pound Brussels sprouts, ends trimmed

1 tablespoon extra-virgin olive oil, divided

Salt

Freshly ground black pepper

1 bunch lacinato kale, or kale of your choice, roughly chopped

1 teaspoon sumac

1 teaspoon toasted sesame seeds

1 tablespoon toasted sunflower seeds

Pomegranate seeds (optional)

TECHNIQUE: Leaving the Brussels sprouts whole for this recipe keeps their integrity and color better. If you cut the Brussels sprouts in half, they get very soft after just one minute of steaming.

4. Remove the steamer basket and set aside. Remove the pressure-cooker pot and trivet, and discard the water. Wipe the pot dry and return it to the cooker.

5. Select the Sauté setting, then add ½ tablespoon of olive oil and the Brussels sprouts to the pressure-cooker pot. Season with salt and pepper, and cook for about 1 minute, until lightly golden brown.

6. Add the remaining ½ tablespoon of olive oil, the kale, and sumac, and sauté for 1 to 2 minutes, until the kale is just barely wilted. Season with salt and pepper.

7. Top with toasted sesame and sunflower seeds, and pomegranate seeds (if using). Serve immediately or at room temperature.

Balsamic Beet, Fennel, Hazelnut, and Goat Cheese Salad

Serves 4 to 6

PREP TIME: 5 MINUTES

MANUAL/PRESSURE COOK: **15 MINUTES HIGH PRESSURE**

RELEASE: **QUICK**

TOTAL TIME: **30 MINUTES**

Beets are gorgeous, flavorful, and so good for you, but they can take over an hour to cook in the oven or on the stove top. The pressure cooker cuts that time down drastically. Adding toasted hazelnuts, crisp fresh fennel, and crumbled goat cheese turns this into a restaurant-worthy dish. A drizzle of good balsamic vinegar and olive oil and a sprinkle of flaky sea salt are the only finishing touches you need.

1. In the pressure-cooker pot, add 1½ cups of water and place a steamer basket inside.

2. Put the beets in the basket. Close and lock the lid.

3. Select the Manual/Pressure Cook setting and cook for 15 minutes at high pressure. When cooking is complete, quick release the pressure. Unlock and carefully remove the lid. If the beets aren't tender enough when pierced with a fork, replace and lock the lid and steam for an additional 2 minutes.

4. Remove the beets from the steamer basket and set aside to cool. When cool enough to handle, peel the skin from the beets. Wear gloves or use paper towels so your hands do not get stained purple. A traditional vegetable peeler works well too.

5. Cut the peeled beets into quarters.

6. In a mixing bowl, toss the beets with the fennel, hazelnuts, goat cheese, vinegar, olive oil, and salt. Serve.

4 medium beets, trimmed

½ bulb fennel, julienned

¼ cup roughly chopped hazelnuts

½ cup crumbled goat cheese

¼ cup balsamic vinegar

2 tablespoons extra-virgin olive oil

Pinch flaky sea salt

TIP: If you don't have fennel or hazelnuts on hand, that's okay, too. Beets and goat cheese are a delicious combo—just add some olive oil, lemon juice, flaky sea salt, and mint, and you're good to go!

Spicy Braised Cabbage

Serves 4

PREP TIME: **5 MINUTES**

MANUAL/PRESSURE COOK: **2 MINUTES HIGH PRESSURE**

RELEASE: **QUICK**

TOTAL TIME: **15 MINUTES**

I love kimchi, but it's labor intensive to make, and you have to wait days for it to ferment before you can eat it. This quick pressure-cooker version delivers that spicy kick I love, thanks to Sriracha, without all the work and waiting. It makes for a great side dish for roasted meats, Korean-Style Short Ribs (page 106), or grilled sausages.

1. In the pressure-cooker pot, whisk together the stock, Sriracha, and salt until just combined. Add the cabbage. Close and lock the lid.

2. Select the Manual/Pressure Cook setting and cook for 2 minutes at high pressure. When cooking is complete, quick release the pressure. Unlock and carefully remove the lid.

3. Season with more salt, if desired, and stir in the scallions. Serve warm, or refrigerate and serve cold.

1 cup Vegetable Stock (page 136)

¼ cup Sriracha hot sauce

2 teaspoons salt, plus more for seasoning

1 small head green cabbage, cored, quartered, and cut into ½-inch-thick slices

3 scallions, sliced

OPTION: If you're not a fan of spice, you can try using sweet chili sauce, which is mildly spicy and adds sweetness. And of course, you can use your own favorite hot sauce if you don't have Sriracha.

Spaghetti Squash

Serves 4

PREP TIME: **15 MINUTES**

MANUAL/PRESSURE COOK: **10 MINUTES HIGH PRESSURE**

RELEASE: **QUICK**

TOTAL TIME: **30 MINUTES**

I like to replace pasta with spaghetti squash, since it's lower in carbohydrates and calories. The shredded squash makes a really satisfying meal when topped with a hearty Bolognese Sauce (page 102) or even just some good olive oil and freshly grated Parmesan cheese.

1 (3-pound) spaghetti squash

Extra-virgin olive oil or butter, for garnish

Freshly grated Parmesan, Romano, Pecorino, or feta cheese, for garnish

Chopped fresh herbs, such as parsley, oregano, or thyme, for garnish

INGREDIENT TIP: I often substitute spaghetti squash for pasta, use it as a base for stews, or serve it as a side with chicken.

1. In the pressure-cooker pot, add 1 cup water and place the trivet inside.

2. Carefully cut the spaghetti squash in half crosswise (not lengthwise) and scoop out the seeds. Cutting it crosswise will produce longer strands.

3. Place the squash halves cut-side up on the trivet. Close and lock the lid.

4. Select the Manual/Pressure Cook setting and cook for 10 minutes at high pressure.

5. When cooking is complete, quick release the pressure. Unlock and carefully open the lid. Use a fork to scrape the inside of the squash to test if it's done. It should be a little al dente, but if it's still crunchy, replace and lock the lid, cook it for a few more minutes, and test again.

6. When done, carefully transfer the squash to a plate or bowl, let cool until it's cool to the touch, and continue to scrape out the strands with the fork. Discard the outer skin once complete.

7. Transfer the squash to a serving plate and garnish with olive oil or butter, cheese, and fresh herbs.

Grandma's Chicken Soup, *page 66*

CHAPTER 5

Soups, Stews & Chilies

The electric pressure cooker is extremely versatile and absolutely ideal for cooking certain foods. These include soups, stews, and chilies. The high-temperature cooking intensifies flavors, tenderizes meats and other ingredients, and does it all in a fraction of the time it would take on the stove top.

The Instant Pot offers Soup/Broth, Beans/Chili, and Meat/Stew settings. Cosori gives you Soup, Beans/Chili, Meat/Stew, and Hot Pot, while the Power Pressure Cooker XL includes a Soup/Stew button.

Shrimp Chupe

Serves 4

PREP TIME: **5 MINUTES**

MANUAL/PRESSURE COOK: **6 MINUTES LOW PRESSURE**

RELEASE: **QUICK**

TOTAL TIME: **20 MINUTES**

½ pound shrimp, deveined and tails removed

½ cup rice

1 cup Fish Stock (page 135) or octopus stock (see Spanish-Style Octopus, page 114)

¼ cup vegetable medley (with corn)

1 tablespoon Sriracha hot sauce

Salt

¼ cup evaporated milk (optional)

This is a take on the Peruvian classic *chupe de camarones*, a thick, chowder-like soup made with shrimp and finished with a rich splash of cream. For the absolute best result, use the broth from the Spanish-Style Octopus recipe (page 114), make your own Fish Stock (page 135), or buy a high-quality fish stock at any fish market. The evaporated milk stirred in before serving is a traditional touch, adding a hint of sweetness and a creamy texture, but you can leave it out if you like—the soup will still be delicious.

TECHNIQUE: The better the stock, the better the soup. Ideally, you can make the Spanish-Style Octopus (page 114) and use the resulting stock to make this chupe, so you're getting two meals in one!

1. In the pressure-cooker pot, combine the shrimp, rice, stock, vegetable medley, and Sriracha. Season with salt. Close and lock the lid.

2. Select the Manual/Pressure Cook setting and cook for 6 minutes at low pressure. When cooking is complete, quick release the pressure. Unlock and carefully remove the lid.

3. Stir in the evaporated milk (if using) and season with salt. Serve.

Clam Chowder

Serves 4 to 6

PREP TIME: **10 MINUTES**

SAUTÉ: **10 MINUTES**

MANUAL/PRESSURE COOK: **2 MINUTES HIGH PRESSURE**

RELEASE: **QUICK**

TOTAL TIME: **30 MINUTES**

This Boston-style chowder will transport you to New England with every spoonful. Using canned clams and the electric pressure cooker makes this an easy meal that can be on the table in just 30 minutes. The flavors of the briny clams, smoky bacon, and fragrant leeks mingle together in an irresistible combo. Crusty bread is the perfect accompaniment.

1. Thinly slice the white part of the leek and place the slices in a bowl of water for 15 minutes. Skim the pieces out of the bowl and pat dry with a paper towel.

2. In the pressure-cooker pot, add the bacon and olive oil. Select the Sauté setting and cook for 10 minutes, until the bacon is golden brown and some of its fat is released.

3. Add the leeks and cook for about 3 minutes, until softened. Add the flour and stir everything well so that you create a roux and the flour cooks. Add the reserved clam juice, clam stock, and potatoes. Close and lock the lid.

4. Select the Manual/Pressure Cook setting and cook for 2 minutes at high pressure. When cooking is complete, quick release the pressure. Unlock and carefully open the lid. Stir in the clams, and the yogurt if desired. Season with salt and pepper. Serve.

1 leek, white part only

4 ounces bacon, sliced into ¼-inch-thick pieces

1 tablespoon extra-virgin olive oil

3 tablespoons all-purpose flour

4 (6-ounce) cans clams, clams drained and juice reserved separately

1 (15-ounce) jar clam stock

2 potatoes, diced

¾ cup plain whole-milk Greek yogurt (optional)

Salt

Freshly ground black pepper

TECHNIQUE: Start the process of sautéing the bacon from a cold pressure-cooker pot so the fat of the bacon starts rendering as the pot heats up. The fat will coat the leeks in step 2, giving you more flavor in the finished soup.

INGREDIENT TIP: Because their leaves grow in tight layers, leeks tend to have a lot of dirt trapped inside them and therefore require extra-thorough cleaning.

Grandma's Chicken Soup

Serves 4 to 6

PREP TIME: **10 MINUTES**

MANUAL/PRESSURE COOK: **20 MINUTES HIGH PRESSURE**

RELEASE: **NATURAL**

TOTAL TIME: **1 HOUR**

My grandmother always said her chicken soup could cure anything, and I believe her. I make it when I feel like I'm about to get a cold, when I have a cold, and, of course, anytime I'm missing Grandma. I don't sauté anything; I just put all the ingredients in the pot and cover them with water. I like to use bone-in, skin-on chicken for an extra-flavorful broth, and then shred all the chicken at the very end. Some of the meat goes back into the soup, and I save the rest for other meals. As with the Whole Chicken (page 84), that extra meat can be used to make Sofrito Chicken Stew (page 86), Shredded Chicken Marinara (page 87), Shredded Chicken in Avocado Salad (page 88), and other dishes.

1. Thinly slice the white part of the leek and place the slices in a bowl of water for 15 minutes. Skim the pieces out of the bowl and pat dry with a paper towel. Wash the dark green leek leaves (if using) in the same bowl or under a faucet, cleaning thoroughly. Tie the leaves together with butcher's twine.

2. In the pressure-cooker pot, arrange the chicken, white leek slices, onion, bell pepper, garlic, and leek leaves or herb stems tied with butcher's twine (if using). Cover with water. Close and lock the lid.

1 leek, white part only

Leek leaves (dark green), or parsley or cilantro stems, tied with butcher's twine so you can easily pull them out

1 whole chicken (about 2 pounds), butchered (ideally with bones and skin, to add more flavor)

1 onion, roughly chopped

1 red bell pepper, roughly chopped

4 garlic cloves, minced

Salt

Freshly ground black pepper

Chopped carrots (optional)

Chopped celery (optional)

Chopped green onions (optional)

Fresh parsley or cilantro leaves, chopped, for garnish (optional)

OPTION: Once the soup is cooked, you can add some egg noodles, switch the pressure cooker to the Sauté function, and cook for another 6 minutes until the noodles are tender.

INGREDIENT TIP: Because their leaves grow in tight layers, leeks tend to have a lot of dirt trapped inside them and therefore require extra-thorough cleaning.

FREEZER TIP: Store the reserved meat and/or leftover soup in airtight containers for up to 3 days in the refrigerator or up to 3 months in the freezer.

3. Select the Manual/Pressure Cook setting and cook for 20 minutes at high pressure. When cooking is complete, allow the pressure to release naturally. Unlock and carefully remove the lid.

4. Remove the leek leaves or herb stems and discard.

5. Gently take the chicken out (it will be falling off the bone) and transfer it to a clean workspace. Shred the chicken with two forks, preserving the meat and discarding the skin and bones.

6. Put 1 or 2 cups of the shredded meat back in your soup and reserve the rest to use in different recipes. Season the soup with salt and pepper and garnish with optional carrots, celery, green onions, chopped parsley or cilantro. Serve.

Farro, Swiss Chard, and Leek Soup

Serves 4 to 6

PREP TIME: **10 MINUTES**

SAUTÉ: **2 MINUTES**

MANUAL/PRESSURE COOK: **10 MINUTES HIGH PRESSURE**

RELEASE: **NATURAL**

TOTAL TIME: **45 MINUTES**

Farro is an ancient grain that's been making a big comeback lately. Like other whole grains, farro is high in fiber and other nutrients, and it makes for a filling and nutritious soup. It contains gluten, but in lower levels than today's wheat, and soaking it and preparing it in an electric pressure cooker makes it easier to digest.

1. Thinly slice the white part of the leek and place the slices in a bowl of water for 15 minutes. Skim the pieces out of the bowl and pat dry with a paper towel.

2. In a small bowl, cover the farro in water and set aside.

3. Select the Sauté function on high, and add the olive oil and leeks to the pressure-cooker pot. Season with salt to help them release some moisture, and cook for about 2 minutes.

4. Add the chard, season with salt, and sauté for about 2 minutes.

5. Add the butter and continue to stir.

6. Drain the farro and add it, along with the chicken stock, to the pot. Close and lock the lid.

7. Select the Manual/Pressure Cook setting and cook for 10 minutes at high pressure. When cooking is complete, allow the pressure to release naturally. Unlock and carefully remove the lid.

8. Season with salt and pepper, and finish the soup off with some balsamic reduction (if using) for extra flavor. Serve.

1 leek, white part only

1 cup farro

2 tablespoons extra-virgin olive oil

Salt

1 bunch rainbow Swiss chard, roughly chopped

1 tablespoon butter

3 cups Chicken Stock (page 134) or Vegetable Stock (page 136)

Freshly ground black pepper

Balsamic reduction, for finishing (optional)

OPTION: If you have extra shredded chicken left over from your Grandma's Chicken Soup (page 66) or Whole Chicken (page 84), add it to the pressure-cooker pot when the soup is done, using the Sauté setting to heat the chicken through.

INGREDIENT TIP: Because their leaves grow in tight layers, leeks tend to have a lot of dirt trapped inside them and therefore require extra-thorough cleaning.

Apricot Chicken Stew

Serves 4

PREP TIME: **5 MINUTES**

MANUAL/PRESSURE COOK: **2 MINUTES HIGH PRESSURE**

RELEASE: **QUICK**

TOTAL TIME: **15 MINUTES**

Apricot preserves and ginger infuse this simple chicken stew with flavor, making it an easy weeknight meal that the whole family will enjoy. I like to serve it with crusty bread for dunking, but you could serve it over rice or pasta instead.

1. In the pressure-cooker pot, combine the chicken thighs, scallions, apricot preserves, ginger, and chicken broth. Close and lock the lid.

2. Select the Manual/Pressure Cook setting and cook for 2 minutes at high pressure. When cooking is complete, quick release the pressure. Unlock and carefully remove the lid.

3. Serve in a large bowl, with crusty bread alongside.

1½ pounds boneless, skinless chicken thighs, halved

1 cup thinly sliced scallions

3 tablespoons apricot preserves

2½ teaspoons ground ginger

1 cup Chicken Stock (page 134) or water

Crusty bread, for serving

OPTION: Change the flavor profile of the dish by swapping in another type of preserve like orange or prune.

Potato and Cheese Locro

Serves 4 to 6

PREP TIME: **10 MINUTES**

SAUTÉ: **5 MINUTES**

MANUAL/PRESSURE COOK: **5 MINUTES HIGH PRESSURE**

RELEASE: **NATURAL**

TOTAL TIME: **35 MINUTES**

Locro de papa is a traditional Ecuadorian soup with a thick potato base. Milk and local cheese are often blended into the soup, adding richness and flavor. If you've never cooked with achiote paste before, I encourage you to seek it out—you can find it in any Latin American market or in the international-foods aisle of many supermarkets. It's a paste made from annatto seeds, garlic, cumin, and other spices. Just a little bit adds loads of flavor to this dish.

1. Select the Sauté setting to preheat the pressure-cooker pot.

2. When hot, add the oil and onion, and cook for 2 minutes until translucent. If the onion begins to brown, reduce the heat to low.

3. Add the garlic, cumin, and achiote paste, and cook for 1 additional minute. Add the potatoes to the pot and mix until well combined, about 1 to 2 minutes. Add the chicken stock and stir. Close and lock the lid.

4. Select the Manual/Pressure Cook setting and cook for 5 minutes at high pressure. When cooking is complete, allow the pressure to release naturally. Unlock and carefully open the lid.

5. Stir in the milk, ¼ cup of cheese (if using), and the cilantro (if using). Season with salt. Garnish with the remaining ¼ cup of cheese (if using). Serve.

2 tablespoons extra-virgin olive oil

½ white onion, diced

1 garlic clove, minced

¼ teaspoon ground cumin

1 teaspoon achiote paste

5 medium russet potatoes, peeled and quartered

4 cups Chicken Stock (page 134)

½ cup whole milk

½ cup grated mozzarella or crumbled cheese (such as queso fresco), divided (optional)

½ bunch fresh cilantro, chopped (optional)

Salt

SUBSTITUTION: Make this dish vegan by using Vegetable Stock (page 136) instead of chicken stock, swapping in nondairy milk, and omitting the cheese.

Tomato Soup

Serves 4

PREP TIME: **5 MINUTES**

MANUAL/PRESSURE COOK: **5 MINUTES LOW PRESSURE**

RELEASE: **NATURAL**

TOTAL TIME: **30 MINUTES**

This simple, home style tomato soup is rich, creamy, and unbelievably easy to make in your electric pressure cooker. I love to serve it with grilled cheese sandwiches on a rainy day for a classic combo guaranteed to make you smile.

1. In the pressure-cooker pot, combine the cherry tomatoes, onion, carrot (if using), vegetable stock, bay leaf, and salt. Close and lock the lid.

2. Select the Manual/Pressure Cook setting and cook for 5 minutes at low pressure. When cooking is complete, allow the pressure to release naturally.

3. Unlock and carefully remove the lid. Discard the bay leaf.

4. Using an immersion blender (or transferring to a standard blender), purée the ingredients until smooth.

5. Stir in the heavy cream and fresh basil. Season with salt. Serve.

2 pints cherry tomatoes

1 medium onion, thinly sliced

1 carrot, chopped (optional)

2 cups Vegetable Stock (page 136) or water

1 bay leaf

1 teaspoon salt

½ cup heavy cream

Fresh basil, chopped or torn, to taste

OPTION: If you like your tomato soup on the sweeter side, be sure to add a carrot. It balances the acidity of the tomatoes and makes the soup sweeter.

Pozole

Serves 6 to 8

PREP TIME: **15 MINUTES**

MANUAL/PRESSURE COOK: **30 MINUTES HIGH PRESSURE**

KEEP WARM: **5 MINUTES**

RELEASE: **NATURAL FOR 15 MINUTES, THEN QUICK**

TOTAL TIME: **1 HOUR 15 MINUTES**

Pozole is to Mexico as ramen is to Japan. Just as ramen noodles are the star ingredient in the Japanese soup, hominy—dried corn soaked in mineral lime—is the key to this Mexican soup. The hominy adds intense corn flavor, and the plump, slightly chewy kernels bring texture to the soup. These days you can find hominy sold in cans in most supermarkets. Once you try pozole, you will forever crave it.

1. Cut the pork into four equal pieces against the grain. In the pressure-cooker pot, combine the pork, onion, garlic, guajillo chiles, and salt.

2. Add 4 cups of water. Close and lock the lid.

3. Select the Manual/Pressure Cook setting and cook for 30 minutes at high pressure. When cooking is complete, allow the pressure to release naturally for 15 minutes, then quick release any remaining pressure. Unlock and carefully open the lid.

4. Transfer the pork pieces to a large bowl. When cool enough to handle, shred the meat with two forks, tongs, or your hands.

5. Use an immersion blender to purée the ingredients in the pressure-cooker pot (or transfer to a standard blender and purée there).

6. Select the Keep Warm setting, and add the shredded meat and hominy to the broth. Stir to combine, and season with salt.

7. Serve immediately, garnished with diced avocado, sliced radishes, lime wedges, and/or fresh cilantro (if using). Alternatively, cool and store in the refrigerator in an airtight container for up to 4 days, or freeze for up to 3 months.

3 pounds pork shoulder, skin off, large pieces of fat trimmed away

1 yellow or white onion, sliced

6 garlic cloves, minced

8 large dried guajillo chiles, stems and seeds removed

2 teaspoons salt, plus more to taste

1 (14-ounce) can hominy, drained

Diced avocado, for garnish (optional)

Sliced radishes, for garnish (optional)

Lime wedges, for garnish (optional)

Fresh cilantro leaves, for garnish (optional)

INGREDIENT TIP: If you can't find hominy, no worries! The soup is still delicious without it.

Latin-Style Black Beans

Serves 6 to 8

PREP TIME: **10 MINUTES**

SAUTÉ: **5 MINUTES**

MANUAL/PRESSURE COOK: **15 MINUTES HIGH PRESSURE**

RELEASE: **NATURAL**

TOTAL TIME: **45 MINUTES**

When I was growing up in Venezuela, this dish was a staple in our house. My grandparents would make it in the old stove-top pressure cooker at least once a week, but it's even quicker and easier to make in the electric pressure cooker. You don't even need to presoak the beans, and they take just 15 minutes to cook. I enjoy eating these beans over rice for an easy, healthy, and inexpensive meal.

1. Select the Sauté setting. If using the bacon, cook for 5 minutes, until browned.

2. Add the sofrito sauce and stir. Season with a pinch of salt.

3. Add the black beans, stock, cumin, and bay leaves. Close and lock the lid.

4. Select the Manual/Pressure Cook setting and cook for 15 minutes at high pressure. When cooking is complete, allow the pressure to release naturally. Unlock and carefully remove the lid.

5. For a creamier consistency, remove 1 cup of beans from the pot and purée them in a blender before adding them back into the pot. Season with salt, and serve.

2 bacon strips, thinly sliced (optional)

1 cup Sofrito Base Sauce (page 140)

Salt

16 ounces dried black beans

4 cups beef stock (see Shredded Beef, page 96), Chicken Stock (page 134), Vegetable Stock (page 136), or water

1 teaspoon ground cumin

2 bay leaves

FREEZER TIP: This recipe makes a large batch of beans, so I like to divide it up and put some in resealable plastic bags to freeze for up to 6 months. Beans always taste better the next day, and they're great when you defrost them, too.

Indian Chickpea Stew

Serves 4

PREP TIME: **5 MINUTES**

MANUAL/PRESSURE COOK: **38 MINUTES HIGH PRESSURE**

RELEASE: **NATURAL**

TOTAL TIME: **1 HOUR**

Garam masala is a wonderful spice mix that typically contains cinnamon, cloves, cardamom, cumin, and other spices. You can substitute another curry powder if you like, but try to find one that contains those key ingredients as well as fenugreek and turmeric. All of these flavors combine to give this simple chickpea stew a real "wow" factor.

1. In the pressure-cooker pot, combine the marinara sauce, chickpeas, garam masala, cumin, fenugreek, and turmeric (if using). Add ¾ cup water. Close and lock the lid.

2. Select the Manual/Pressure Cook setting and cook for 38 minutes at high pressure. When cooking is complete, allow the pressure to release naturally. Unlock and carefully remove the lid. Season with salt, and serve.

1½ cups Marinara Sauce (page 139)

1 cup dried chickpeas

1 teaspoon garam masala

1 teaspoon ground cumin

1 teaspoon ground fenugreek

1 teaspoon ground turmeric (optional)

OPTION: You can fold in some spinach or cilantro at the end for a bit of color and flavor.

Spanish-Style Lentils with Chorizo

Serves 4 to 6

PREP TIME: **5 MINUTES**

SAUTÉ: **2 MINUTES**

MANUAL/PRESSURE COOK: **13 MINUTES HIGH PRESSURE**

RELEASE: **NATURAL FOR 10 MINUTES, THEN QUICK**

TOTAL TIME: **40 MINUTES**

I adore lentils, not least because they're so easy to make in the electric pressure cooker. This simple recipe takes less than an hour from start to finish, but its depth of flavor will surprise you. If you don't have sofrito ready to go, simply add half a diced onion, half a diced bell pepper, and two minced garlic cloves to the pot along with the chorizo.

1. Select the Sauté setting to preheat the pressure-cooker pot. When hot, add the olive oil and chorizo. Sauté about 1 minute, then add the sofrito. Cook for 1 additional minute, stirring regularly.

2. Add the lentils, chicken stock, and a pinch of salt. Close and lock the lid.

3. Select the Manual/Pressure Cook setting and cook for 13 minutes at high pressure. When cooking is complete, allow the pressure to release naturally for 10 minutes, then quick release any remaining pressure.

4. Unlock and carefully remove the lid. Season with salt and pepper. Serve.

1 tablespoon extra-virgin olive oil

½ pound chorizo sausage (or sausage of your choice), casing removed, diced

¼ cup Sofrito Base Sauce (page 140)

1 cup dried green lentils, rinsed

3 cups Chicken Stock (page 134) or water

Salt

Freshly ground black pepper

OPTION: For a thicker consistency, remove 1 cup of the soup, purée it in a blender, and fold it back into the remaining lentils.

Collard Greens Stew with Cannellini Beans and Ham Hocks

Serves 4

PREP TIME: 10 MINUTES

MANUAL/PRESSURE COOK: **28 MINUTES HIGH PRESSURE**

RELEASE: **NATURAL**

TOTAL TIME: **1 HOUR**

Collard greens are a classic American leafy green vegetable. They're known for needing a long time to cook, but the electric pressure cooker turns out perfectly tender greens in about an hour. Cannellini beans and smoked ham hocks give this stew both depth of flavor and a satisfying texture. Serve with slices of cornbread that can be used to soak up the rich broth.

1. In the pressure-cooker pot, combine the collard green leaves and stems, beans, onions, garlic powder, and 4 cups water. Season with salt and stir well. Nestle the ham hocks on top of the greens. Close and lock the lid.

2. Select the Manual/Pressure Cook setting and cook for 28 minutes at high pressure. When cooking is complete, allow the pressure to release naturally. Unlock and carefully remove the lid.

3. Transfer the ham hocks to a bowl. Shred the meat, then add it back into the stew. Season to taste with salt. Serve.

4 cups collard greens, leaves separated and chopped, stems diced

1 cup dried cannellini beans

2 yellow or white onions, diced

2 teaspoons garlic powder

Salt

2 ham hocks

OPTION: If you'd like, you can serve this stew with a lemon wedge for a bit of brightness.

Beef and Barley Stew

Serves 6

PREP TIME: **10 MINUTES**

SAUTÉ: **11 MINUTES**

MANUAL/PRESSURE COOK: **14 MINUTES HIGH PRESSURE**

RELEASE: **NATURAL FOR 10 MINUTES, THEN QUICK**

KEEP WARM: **15 MINUTES**

TOTAL TIME: **1 HOUR 10 MINUTES**

Warm and hearty, this stew is perfect for a winter day when the kids are home from school. Barley is a high-fiber, high-protein grain with lots of health benefits. Be sure to pull the frozen vegetables from your freezer at the beginning of your preparation, so they'll be defrosted enough to cook quickly once you're ready to add them to the pot.

2 pounds beef chuck or round, cut into 1-inch cubes

Salt

Freshly ground black pepper

2 tablespoons extra-virgin olive oil, divided

1 small yellow onion, finely diced

¾ cup pearl barley

4½ cups beef stock (see Shredded Beef, page 96) or water

5 thyme sprigs

2 cups frozen pea-and-carrot medley, thawed

OPTION: You can use couscous, rice, or pasta if you can't find barley; just check the charts beginning on page 147 and adjust the time accordingly.

1. Select the Sauté setting to preheat the pressure-cooker pot.

2. Season the beef with salt and pepper on all sides. When the cooker is hot, add 1 tablespoon of olive oil and sear half the beef on all sides, about 3 minutes. Transfer the beef to a plate and sear the remaining batch with the remaining 1 tablespoon of olive oil. Transfer that batch to a plate as well.

3. In the pressure-cooker pot, add the onion and sauté about 2 minutes, until translucent. Add the seared beef and any juices from the plate, as well as the barley, beef stock, and thyme sprigs. Close and lock the lid.

4. Select the Manual/Pressure Cook setting and cook for 14 minutes at high pressure. When cooking is complete, allow the pressure to release naturally for 10 minutes, then quick release any remaining pressure. Unlock and carefully remove the lid.

5. Stir in the pea-and-carrot medley. Select the Sauté setting and cook for 3 minutes, to heat the peas and carrots through.

6. Remove and discard the thyme sprigs, season with salt, and turn the cooker to Keep Warm. Let sit for 15 minutes to let the barley fully soak up the liquid. Serve.

Ground Turkey Chili with Red Kidney Beans and Chipotle

Serves 4

PREP TIME: **15 MINUTES**
SAUTÉ: **10 MINUTES**
MANUAL/PRESSURE COOK: **30 MINUTES HIGH PRESSURE**
RELEASE: **NATURAL**
TOTAL TIME: **1 HOUR 10 MINUTES**

Spiced up with chipotle chiles in adobo sauce, this ground turkey chili explodes with flavor. Top it with ground turkey chili toppings—shredded cheese, sour cream, tortilla chips—for a great family meal. The leftovers make a fantastic burrito filling, too.

1. In the pressure-cooker pot, add the olive oil, onion, and a pinch of salt. Select the Sauté setting and sweat the onion for about 3 minutes.

2. Add the ground turkey along with 1 tablespoon of chipotle. Cook for 5 minutes. With a slotted spoon, transfer the onion-and-turkey mixture to a bowl.

3. Turn off the cooker. Add the flour to the pressure-cooker pot and stir with a wooden spoon. (You're looking to cook the flour a bit, and there will be enough residual heat to do so.)

4. Whisk in the chicken stock, then add the beans, thyme sprigs, and the remaining 1 tablespoon of chipotle. Close and lock the lid.

5. Select the Manual/Pressure Cook setting and cook for 30 minutes at high pressure. When cooking is complete, allow the pressure to release naturally. Unlock and carefully open the lid.

6. Stir in the onion-and-turkey mixture, remove and discard the thyme sprigs, and serve.

1 tablespoon extra-virgin olive oil

1 onion, diced

Salt

1 pound ground turkey

2 tablespoons minced chipotle in adobo, divided

2 tablespoons all-purpose flour

2 cups Chicken Stock (page 134) or water

1½ cups dried red kidney beans

4 fresh thyme sprigs

Shredded Cheddar cheese, for serving (optional)

Sour cream, for serving (optional)

Tortilla chips, for serving (optional)

TECHNIQUE: When cooking something hearty in a pressure cooker, you want to build flavor. Take the time to sauté the turkey and onions well in order to build on the flavor profiles. For a creamier mouthfeel, garnish with sour cream or cheese.

Thai Green Curry with Lamb

Serves 4

PREP TIME: **10 MINUTES**

SAUTÉ: **4 MINUTES**

MANUAL/PRESSURE COOK: **12 MINUTES HIGH PRESSURE**

RELEASE: **QUICK**

TOTAL TIME: **35 MINUTES**

- -

The strong flavors of green curry and coconut milk make this a great dish even for people who shy away from lamb because of its sometimes strong flavor. If that's you, ask your butcher for young lamb, which has a milder taste. Add more or less curry paste depending on how spicy you like your food.

1. Select the Sauté setting to preheat the pressure-cooker pot.

2. Season the lamb with salt. When the pressure-cooker pot is hot, add the lamb, olive oil, and green curry paste. Sauté for about 1 minute.

3. Add the potato, coconut milk, and stock. Close and lock the lid.

4. Select Manual/Pressure Cook and cook for 12 minutes at high pressure. When cooking is complete, quick release the pressure. Unlock and carefully remove the lid.

5. Transfer the lamb pieces to a serving bowl.

6. Set the cooker to Sauté again, and add the green beans. Cook for 2 to 3 minutes, until the beans are just tender. Season with salt.

7. Pour the curry sauce over the lamb. Top with fresh chopped basil and mint (if using), and serve.

2 pounds lamb stew meat, cut into 2-inch cubes

Salt

2 tablespoons extra-virgin olive oil

4 tablespoons green curry paste

1 russet potato, peeled and diced roughly into ½-inch chunks

1 (13.5-ounce) can coconut milk

1 cup beef stock (see Shredded Beef, page 96)

¾ pound green beans, cut into 1-inch segments

2 tablespoons chopped fresh basil or Thai basil leaves, for garnish (optional)

2 tablespoons chopped fresh mint leaves, for garnish (optional)

OPTION: I highly encourage you to squeeze some fresh lime juice onto this dish before eating it, as it will wake up the dish and brighten all the flavors.

Arroz con Pollo, *page 89*

CHAPTER 6

Main Meals

The electric pressure cooker is great for cooking meats, especially tougher cuts, which become delightfully tender during pressure cooking. It also works well for leaner, more delicate proteins like chicken and fish as long as you're careful not to overcook them. Vegetables, too, can be cooked in the pressure cooker, especially sturdier ones like root vegetables and artichokes.

The Power Pressure Cooker XL has a Chicken/Meat button as well as a Fish/Vegetables Steam button. The Instant Pot gives you Meat/Stew, and the Cosori offers Meat/Stew and Poultry buttons.

Continued

Chicken Tikka Masala

Serves 4

PREP TIME: **10 MINUTES**

SAUTÉ: **4 MINUTES**

POULTRY OR MANUAL/PRESSURE COOK: **3 MINUTES HIGH PRESSURE**

RELEASE: **QUICK**

TOTAL TIME: **30 MINUTES**

Chicken tikka masala's origin story is a bit controversial. We think of it as Indian food, but it may well have been created in the United Kingdom. Wherever it originated, it is now an American favorite, and it's perfectly suited to cooking in the pressure cooker. The trick is finding a good tikka masala sauce, but don't worry, there are some great ones out there.

1. Select the Sauté setting to preheat the pressure-cooker pot. Add the onion and season with salt to help it release moisture. Sauté until slightly caramelized, about 3 minutes.

2. Add the tomato paste and stir for 1 minute. Deglaze with the stock, scraping up any browned bits off the bottom of the pot.

3. Add the chicken and tikka masala sauce. Close and lock the lid.

4. Select the Poultry or Manual/Pressure Cook setting and cook for 3 minutes at high pressure. When cooking is complete, quick release the pressure. Carefully unlock and remove the lid.

5. Fold in the coconut milk or yogurt. Garnish with chopped cilantro (if using). Serve.

½ red onion, thinly sliced

Salt

2 tablespoons tomato paste

¼ cup Chicken Stock (page 134) or water

1½ pounds bone-in chicken thighs, skin removed

1 (15-ounce) jar tikka masala sauce

1 cup coconut milk or full-fat Greek yogurt

Fresh cilantro leaves, chopped, for garnish (optional)

INGREDIENT TIP: Tikka masala sauce is sold in many specialty grocery stores, Asian markets, and Indian markets. Look for it in the bottled or canned food section, or if it's unavailable where you live, find it online.

Whole Chicken

Serves 4 to 6

PREP TIME: **10 MINUTES**

MANUAL/PRESSURE COOK: **20 MINUTES HIGH PRESSURE**

RELEASE: **QUICK**

TOTAL TIME: **45 MINUTES**

I love cooking a whole chicken because you can eat it for dinner "as is" one night, then use the leftovers for all sorts of other dishes later in the week. I use shredded leftover chicken from this recipe for Sofrito Chicken Stew (page 86), or toss it with Marinara Sauce (page 139) and pasta. It's also perfect for the Shredded Chicken in Avocado Salad (page 88), as a chicken salad for sandwiches, or tossed into a green salad to make it a meal. Save the carcass of the chicken after you've shredded the meat; you can use it to make a flavorful homemade Chicken Stock (page 134).

1. Chop 1 tablespoon of thyme leaves (from about 5 sprigs), and in a small bowl, mix with the mustard.

2. Remove the liver and gizzards from the chicken cavity. Detach the chicken skin from the flesh to create a pocket, and smear the mustard-and-thyme mixture between the flesh and the skin of the chicken. Season the outside skin of the chicken with salt and pepper on all sides.

10 thyme sprigs, divided

3 tablespoons Dijon or honey mustard

1 whole chicken (about 4 pounds)

Salt

Freshly ground black pepper

1 onion, roughly diced

2 celery stalks, roughly diced

MAKE-AHEAD TIP: You can make three completely different meals from the meat of this one chicken. If you wish to freeze the meat for later use, I suggest shredding it and freezing it with a bit of stock so it doesn't dry out. Cooking the chicken also releases some very flavorful juices that you should save and use as stock. Just strain and skim the stock, transfer it to an airtight container, and refrigerate it for up to 1 week or freeze it for up to 3 months.

3. In the pressure-cooker pot, arrange the onion and celery on the bottom. Nestle the chicken inside the pot. Add 1 cup of water, and place the remaining thyme sprigs in the liquid. Close and lock the lid.

4. Select the Manual/Pressure Cook setting and cook for 20 minutes at high pressure. (A good guide to cooking time is 5 minutes per pound of chicken.) When cooking is complete, quick release the pressure. Unlock and carefully remove the lid.

5. Carefully remove the chicken from the pressure cooker and transfer it to a cutting board or large bowl. Strain and reserve the cooking liquid—this is excellent chicken broth! Carve the chicken and serve immediately. Or, for shredded chicken, when the meat is cool enough to handle, use two forks or your hands to shred it.

Sofrito Chicken Stew

Serves 4

PREP TIME: **5 MINUTES**

MANUAL/PRESSURE COOK: **20 MINUTES HIGH PRESSURE**

RELEASE: **NATURAL**

TOTAL TIME: **45 MINUTES**

This was my favorite dish when I was growing up, and it still reminds me of my grandmother. These days, I make it at least once a week, and I never get tired of it because it has so many layers of flavor—the savory sofrito sauce, plus the tangy olives and capers. I like to use drumsticks because dark meat is so juicy and flavorful; chicken thighs work as well. Breasts are fine, too, but you'll want to shorten the cooking time a bit. You can even use leftover cooked chicken from your Whole Chicken (page 84) and save even more time. Ladle this stew over rice so that you catch all the juicy goodness when you eat it.

1. In a mixing bowl, season the chicken with the adobo and pepper.

2. In the pressure-cooker pot, add the chicken drumsticks, sofrito, chicken stock, mustard, olives, and, if desired, the capers. Close and lock the lid.

3. Select the Manual/Pressure Cook setting and cook for 20 minutes at high pressure. When cooking is complete, allow the pressure to release naturally. Unlock and carefully remove the lid.

4. Fold in the cilantro (if using). Season with salt. Serve over rice (if desired).

12 skinless chicken drumsticks

1 teaspoon Goya adobo seasoning

Freshly ground black pepper

1½ cups Sofrito Base Sauce (page 140)

½ cup Chicken Stock (page 134)

1 tablespoon Dijon mustard

2 tablespoons halved, pitted manzanilla olives with pimientos

1 tablespoon capers, drained (optional)

Fresh cilantro leaves, chopped, for garnish (optional)

Salt

Cooked rice, for serving (optional)

OPTION: If you have a bit more time and want to achieve another layer of flavor, you can use the Sauté function of the pressure cooker to slightly brown the chicken drumsticks before adding the rest of the ingredients. To do this, preheat the cooker and, working in batches, use 1 to 2 tablespoons of oil to brown all the sides of the chicken. Alternatively, you can use the shredded chicken from the Chicken Stock (page 134) or Whole Chicken (page 84) to make this dish. Simply fold it into the sofrito sauce, add the rest of the ingredients, heat it up, and you're ready to eat.

Shredded Chicken Marinara

Serves 4

PREP TIME: **5 MINUTES**

POULTRY OR MANUAL/PRESSURE COOK: **3 MINUTES HIGH PRESSURE**

RELEASE: **QUICK**

TOTAL TIME: **20 MINUTES**

This chicken marinara dish is a perfect weeknight meal, as it allows you to repurpose and use leftover shredded chicken from the Whole Chicken (page 84) or Chicken Stock (page 134) recipe. Simply throw all the ingredients in the electric pressure cooker, and you'll have a satisfying dinner in way less time than you would if you were prepping on the stove top.

1. In the pressure-cooker pot, combine the shredded chicken, penne pasta, marinara sauce, and chicken stock. Season with salt and pepper.

2. Select the Poultry or Manual/Pressure Cook setting and cook for 3 minutes at high pressure. When cooking is complete, quick release the pressure. Carefully unlock and remove the lid.

3. To serve, add the Parmesan, chopped fresh herbs (if using), and salt and pepper to taste.

3 cups shredded chicken (see Whole Chicken, page 84)

3 cups penny pasta

2 cups Marinara Sauce (page 139)

1 cup Chicken Stock (page 134)

Salt

Freshly ground black pepper

½ cup grated Parmesan cheese

Fresh parsley or basil leaves, chopped (optional)

SUBSTITUTION: If you don't have leftover shredded chicken, you can simply throw a fresh, uncooked chicken breast (seasoned with salt and pepper) in the pot with the rest of the ingredients and cook per the recipe instructions. Once it's done, take out the chicken breast, shred it with a fork, and mix the shredded chicken back into the pot.

Shredded Chicken in Avocado Salad

Serves 4 to 6

PREP TIME: **5 MINUTES**

I grew up eating shredded chicken instead of chopped—I think it must be a Latin thing. If you have any chicken left over after making a Whole Chicken (page 84), shred it, tuck it in the fridge, and use it for this recipe. In Venezuela, where I grew up, this "salad" is called *reina pepiada* and is used as a filling for arepas or sandwiches, or served on top of cassava bread or salads.

In a medium bowl, combine the avocado, lime juice, mayonnaise, chicken, cilantro (if using), and jalapeño (if using). Mix until just combined. Season with salt and pepper. Serve.

1 ripe avocado, pitted, peeled, and mashed

½ teaspoon lime juice

1 tablespoon mayonnaise

½ cup shredded chicken (see Whole Chicken, page 84)

Fresh cilantro leaves, chopped, for garnish (optional)

Jalapeño, finely chopped (optional)

Salt

Freshly ground black pepper

OPTION: Fill arepas with this salad, serve it on top of cassava bread, or use it in a sandwich or salad.

Arroz con Pollo

Serves 4

PREP TIME: **10 MINUTES**

SAUTÉ: **5 MINUTES**

RICE/PRESSURE COOK: **10 MINUTES HIGH PRESSURE**

MANUAL/PRESSURE COOK: **2 MINUTES HIGH PRESSURE**

RELEASE: **QUICK**

TOTAL TIME: **40 MINUTES**

Every country in Latin America has its own version of this chicken-and-rice dish. It's a great one-pot meal with rice, meat, and veggies that can really stretch your meal dollars while also providing amazing flavor. You won't feel like you're scrimping when you eat this! The recipe calls for achiote paste, which is a mixture of ground annatto seeds, cumin, garlic, and other spices. I recommend the Goya brand. A small amount of this condiment gives the dish its intense and distinctive flavor.

1. In a large bowl, season the chicken with salt and pepper.

2. Select the Sauté setting to preheat the pressure-cooker pot.

3. When hot, add the achiote paste and olive oil, and sear the chicken pieces on all sides, about 5 minutes.

4. Add the rice, sofrito, chicken stock, 1 teaspoon salt, and ¼ teaspoon black pepper. Stir to ensure the rice is fully covered with liquid. Close and lock the lid.

5. Select the Rice/Pressure Cook setting and cook for 10 minutes at high pressure. When cooking is complete, quick release the pressure. Unlock and carefully open the lid.

6. Add the carrots and peas. Close and lock the lid.

7. Select the Manual/Pressure Cook setting and cook for 2 minutes at high pressure. When cooking is complete, quick release the pressure. Carefully unlock and remove the lid. Stir to combine everything. Add cilantro and lemon juice (if using), and serve.

2 pounds chicken drumsticks and/or thighs, skin removed

Salt

Freshly ground black pepper

1½ tablespoons achiote paste

1 tablespoon extra-virgin olive oil

1 cup jasmine rice

½ cup Sofrito Base Sauce (page 140) or Marinara Sauce (see page 139)

1½ cups Chicken Stock (page 134) or water

1 cup frozen carrot-and-pea medley, thawed

Fresh cilantro or parsley leaves, chopped, for serving (optional)

Lemon juice, for serving (optional)

SUBSTITUTION: If you can't get achiote paste, use 3 or 4 crushed saffron threads in its place, and increase the olive oil to 2 tablespoons. Depending on the amount and type of salt you use, you may also need to adjust the salt measurement slightly for this variation.

SUBSTITUTION: Use 1 cup of your favorite IPA beer in place of 1 cup of the stock for a delicious alternative. Finish the dish with some chopped parsley or cilantro and a squeeze of fresh lemon juice to brighten everything up at the end of cooking.

Sweet-and-Sour Chicken

Serves 4

PREP TIME: **10 MINUTES**

SAUTÉ: **6 MINUTES**

POULTRY OR MANUAL/PRESSURE COOK: **5 TO 12 MINUTES HIGH PRESSURE**

RELEASE: **QUICK**

KEEP WARM: **1 MINUTE**

TOTAL TIME: **30 TO 40 MINUTES**

This Asian-style chicken dish was a favorite in my household when I was growing up. Most restaurant versions start out by deep-frying the chicken chunks, but using an electric pressure cooker instead is both quicker and healthier. If you want to serve it over rice, you can prepare the rice in your pressure cooker beforehand, then transfer it to another bowl and cover it with a clean dish towel to keep it warm while the chicken cooks.

1. Select the Sauté setting to preheat the pressure-cooker pot.

2. When hot, add 1 tablespoon oil and sauté the bell pepper for 2 minutes. Season with salt. Remove the bell pepper and transfer it to a plate.

3. Season the chicken with salt. Add ½ tablespoon of oil to the pressure-cooker pot and sear half the chicken pieces, being careful not to crowd the pot, about 2 minutes.

2 tablespoons sesame oil or canola oil, divided

1 large red bell pepper, cut into 1-inch pieces

Salt

1½ pounds boneless, skinless chicken breast, cut into 2-inch chunks, or bone-in chicken thighs, skin removed

1 (16-ounce) jar sweet-and-sour sauce

1 (20-ounce) can pineapple chunks in juice, juice strained and reserved

Cooked rice or noodles, for serving (optional)

TECHNIQUE: I like to fold in the pineapple at the end instead of cooking it. This preserves the pineapple's texture instead of making it mushy, so you get that extra bite that a nice chunk of pineapple provides.

4. Transfer the chicken to a separate plate and sear the second batch of chicken with the remaining ½ tablespoon of oil. Return all the chicken to the pressure-cooker pot.

5. In the pressure-cooker pot, add the sweet-and-sour sauce and ¾ cup reserved pineapple juice. Stir to combine. Close and lock the lid.

6. Select the Poultry or Manual/Pressure Cook setting and cook for 5 to 8 minutes at high pressure (for chicken breasts) or 10 to 12 minutes at high pressure (for chicken thighs). When cooking is complete, quick release the pressure. (If you're using thighs, natural release works as well.) Carefully unlock and remove the lid.

7. Select the Keep Warm setting and add in the pineapple chunks and reserved bell pepper. Stir to combine and heat through, about 1 minute. Season with salt. Serve over rice or noodles (if desired).

Easy Mole Chicken

Serves 4

PREP TIME: **5 MINUTES**

SAUTÉ: **2 MINUTES**

POULTRY OR MANUAL/PRESSURE COOK: **8 MINUTES HIGH PRESSURE**

RELEASE: **QUICK**

TOTAL TIME: **30 MINUTES**

Mole is the generic name for a number of complex Mexican sauces that can include nuts, spices, dried chiles, and more. The version you find most commonly in Mexican restaurants in the United States also includes dark chocolate. To make a good mole from scratch requires a long list of ingredients and literally hours in the kitchen. For this quick and easy version, I use jarred mole sauce, which you can find in most supermarkets, in Latin American markets, or online. Serve it over rice for a meal the whole family will love.

1. Select the Sauté setting to preheat the pressure-cooker pot.

2. In a large bowl, season the chicken with salt and pepper.

3. When the cooker is hot, add the oil and sear the chicken, about 1 minute on each side.

4. Meanwhile, in a small bowl, whisk together the mole sauce and chicken stock until combined. In the pressure-cooker pot, pour the sauce over the chicken. Close and lock the lid.

5. Select the Poultry or Manual/Pressure Cook setting and cook for 8 minutes at high pressure. When cooking is complete, quick release the pressure. Carefully unlock and remove the lid.

6. Transfer the chicken and sauce to a serving dish, and garnish with sesame seeds (if using). Serve with tortillas and/or rice.

2 pounds bone-in chicken thighs (4 to 6 pieces), skin removed

Salt

Freshly ground black pepper

2 tablespoons extra-virgin olive oil

4 ounces store-bought mole sauce

2 cups Chicken Stock (page 134) or water

Toasted sesame seeds, for garnish (optional)

Tortillas and/or cooked white rice, for serving

OPTION: After removing the chicken, set the cooker to Sauté and reduce the sauce for about 2 minutes for a thicker sauce. I highly encourage you to add the sesame seeds on top for added flavor.

Creamy Ranch Chicken

Serves 4

PREP TIME: **5 MINUTES**

MANUAL/PRESSURE COOK: **5 TO 12 MINUTES HIGH PRESSURE**

RELEASE: **QUICK**

KEEP WARM: **2 MINUTES**

TOTAL TIME: **20 TO 30 MINUTES**

Everyone loves a creamy ranch dressing, right? I love to use packets of ranch dressing mix and cream cheese to make a decadently creamy yet super easy chicken dinner. Adding a sprinkling of fresh herbs and a squeeze of lemon juice just before serving makes the dish taste super fresh. Be sure to take the cream cheese out of the refrigerator at the beginning of your preparation so that it can come up to room temperature. This will make it easier to whisk it into the sauce in the pot.

1. Season the chicken with half of the ranch seasoning packet and the salt.

2. In the pressure-cooker pot, combine the chicken stock and the remaining half of the ranch packet. Place the chicken on top. Close and lock the lid.

3. Select the Manual/Pressure Cook setting and cook for 5 to 8 minutes at high pressure (for chicken breasts) or 10 to 12 minutes at high pressure (for thighs). When cooking is complete, quick release the pressure. (For thighs, natural release works as well.) Carefully unlock and remove the lid.

4. Transfer the chicken breasts to a serving platter.

5. Adjust the cooker to Keep Warm and add the cream cheese pieces to the pressure-cooker pot. Whisk until creamy and fully incorporated, about 2 minutes.

6. Ladle the creamy sauce onto the chicken breasts. Garnish with the fresh chopped herbs (if using). Serve.

30 **Q** **F** **K**

4 boneless, skinless chicken breasts, each about ¾ inch thick, or bone-in chicken thighs, skin removed

1 (1-ounce) packet ranch seasoning mix, divided

½ tablespoon salt

1 cup Chicken Stock (page 134) or water

8 ounces cream cheese, cut into 8 pieces, at room temperature

Fresh dill, parsley, or chives, chopped (optional)

TECHNIQUE: You can season the ranch dressing to taste with salt and pepper before putting in the chicken, if desired.

Chicken Chilaquiles

Serves 4 to 6

PREP TIME: **10 MINUTES**

MANUAL/PRESSURE COOK: **2 MINUTES HIGH PRESSURE**

RELEASE: **QUICK**

TOTAL TIME: **15 MINUTES**

Chilaquiles are a Mexican dish made of tortilla chips cooked with chunks of chicken and tangy-spicy Salsa Verde (page 138). Basically, they're like nachos, only better. Some of the chips stay crispy, while others soak up the sauce. I like to say chilaquiles are the cousin you never met, and then you meet him, and you love him, and you ask yourself, "How did I ever live without him?" They'll change your life for the better.

1. In the pressure-cooker pot, combine the chicken, salsa verde, stock, and corn tortillas. Stir to combine. Close and lock the lid.

2. Select the Manual/Pressure Cook setting and cook for 2 minutes at high pressure. When cooking is complete, quick release the pressure. Carefully unlock and remove the lid.

3. Arrange half the tortilla chips on a serving platter. Mix the remaining tortilla chips into the chicken mixture, and then immediately pour the chicken mixture over the tortilla chips on the serving platter. If using, garnish with queso fresco, chopped cilantro, and/or sliced avocado. Serve.

2 cups shredded chicken (see Whole Chicken, page 84)

1 cup Salsa Verde (page 138)

½ cup Chicken Stock (page 134) or water

4 corn tortillas, torn into four pieces each

3 cups tortilla chips, divided

Herby Queso Fresco (page 36), for garnish (optional)

Fresh cilantro leaves, chopped, for garnish (optional)

Sliced avocado, for garnish (optional)

TECHNIQUE: With chilaquiles, the idea is that some of the chips are soft while others remain crispy, so it tastes like a mixture of nachos and tortilla soup. You can add more sauce if you like, as well as chopped jalapeños if you like more heat.

2-Minute Buffalo Chicken Tenders

Serves 4 to 6

PREP TIME: **5 MINUTES**

MANUAL/PRESSURE COOK: **2 MINUTES HIGH PRESSURE**

SAUTÉ: **3 MINUTES**

RELEASE: **QUICK**

TOTAL TIME: **15 MINUTES**

2 pounds chicken tenders

¾ cup mild red hot sauce

6 tablespoons butter, cut into 6 slices

1½ tablespoons cornstarch

Salt

Blue cheese dressing, for serving

Celery sticks, for serving (optional)

Carrot sticks, for serving (optional)

This quick recipe turns chicken tenders into a flavorful meal with all the delicious flavors of Buffalo wings but none of the mess or fat of deep frying. I love to eat this chicken as a snack-like meal with a blue cheese dip, or put it on top of a green salad with blue cheese dressing.

1. In the pressure-cooker pot, mix the chicken and hot sauce to coat well. Close and lock the lid.

2. Select the Manual/Pressure Cook setting and cook for 2 minutes at high pressure. When cooking is complete, quick release the pressure. Carefully unlock and remove the lid.

3. Remove the chicken tenders from the pot and set aside. Adjust the setting to Sauté for 3 minutes. Whisk in the butter, one pat at a time, until melted.

4. In a small bowl, whisk the cornstarch with 5 tablespoons of the chicken sauce from the pot to make a slurry. Whisk the slurry back into the pressure-cooker pot to thicken the sauce.

5. Put the chicken back in the pressure-cooker pot and stir to coat. Transfer to a plate, and serve with your favorite blue cheese dressing, and optional celery sticks and carrot sticks.

INGREDIENT TIP: Use your favorite hot sauce, ideally something red because that's going to translate into great color in your dish. And remember, if the hot sauce is too hot, then you won't want to eat the dish, so choose a mild one if that suits you—mild goes best with this recipe anyway.

Shredded Beef

Serves 6 to 8

PREP TIME: **5 MINUTES**

MANUAL/PRESSURE COOK: **40 MINUTES AT HIGH PRESSURE**

RELEASE: **NATURAL**

TOTAL TIME: **1 HOUR**

Shredded beef is used in myriad ways in Latin American cuisine. I love to make a large batch and use it over the course of several days—and not just in Latin food, either! This basic recipe makes a batch large enough to enjoy in several meals, including the four recipes that follow: Beef Stroganoff (page 97), Carne Mechada (page 98), Vaca Frita (page 99), and Beef and Broccoli (page 103). It also makes a wonderful beef stock that can be used to enrich soups, stews, and chilies with loads of flavor.

1. In the pressure-cooker pot, combine the flank steak, onion, garlic, bay leaves, salt, leek greens or celery (if using), and 5 cups of water. If the steak won't fit flat, fold it or cut it in half. (You'll be shredding it later, anyway.) Close and lock the lid.

2. Select the Manual/Pressure Cook setting and cook for 40 minutes at high pressure. When cooking is complete, allow the pressure to naturally release. Unlock and carefully remove the lid.

3. Transfer the steak to a large bowl. When cooled slightly, shred the meat with two forks or your hands. Use immediately, or transfer to airtight storage containers and store in the refrigerator for 3 to 4 days or in the freezer for up to 1 month.

4. Place a large sieve over a bowl, and pour the beef stock from the pressure-cooker pot into it. Let cool for about 30 minutes, then transfer to storage containers. Cover and refrigerate for 3 to 4 days, or freeze for up to 1 month.

1 (2-pound) flank steak

1 white or yellow onion, roughly chopped

4 garlic cloves, smashed

2 bay leaves

1 teaspoon salt, plus more for seasoning

2 leek greens or 2 celery stalks, roughly chopped (optional)

MAKE-AHEAD TIP: The beef stock this recipe produces is great to make ahead and use in other recipes. Freezing it in small containers as needed for recipes allows you to quickly pop the stock out of the freezer and have it ready to go in minutes.

INGREDIENT TIP: Because their leaves grow in tight layers, leeks tend to have a lot of dirt trapped inside them and therefore require extra-thorough cleaning. Make sure you've removed all traces of dirt on the leek greens before you add them to the pot.

Beef Stroganoff

Serves 4

PREP TIME: **10 MINUTES**

SAUTÉ: **6 MINUTES**

MANUAL/PRESSURE COOK: **2 MINUTES HIGH PRESSURE**

RELEASE: **QUICK**

TOTAL TIME: **20 MINUTES**

If you've already got a batch of Shredded Beef (page 96), this comforting meal is only minutes away. But even if you haven't precooked the beef, you can start with chunks of raw flank steak, add an extra 10 minutes of cooking time, and you'll have a beautiful, warming beef Stroganoff in no time.

1. Select the Sauté setting to preheat the pressure-cooker pot.

2. When hot, add the olive oil and mushrooms, and cook for 2 minutes. Add the onion and cook for an additional 4 minutes, until the onion is softened and translucent. Season with salt and pepper.

3. Add the beef stock or water to deglaze the pot, using a wooden spoon to scrape any bits of flavor off the bottom of the pot. Add the beef and egg noodles. Close and lock the lid.

4. Select the Manual/Pressure Cook setting and cook for 2 minutes at high pressure. When cooking is complete, quick release the pressure. Unlock and carefully remove the lid.

5. Transfer the pressure-cooker pot to a heatproof surface and let it cool down for about 5 minutes. Fold in the sour cream, and season to taste. Serve.

2 tablespoons extra-virgin olive oil

6 ounces button mushrooms, quartered

1 cup finely diced onion

Salt

Freshly ground black pepper

2 cups beef stock (see Shredded Beef, page 96) or water

1½ cups Shredded Beef (page 96)

2 cups egg noodles

½ cup sour cream

TECHNIQUE: Let the sauce cool a bit before adding the sour cream. This prevents the sauce from breaking (or separating), which would make the final dish less creamy than you want it to be. If you're starting with raw flank steak, cook the steak for 8 minutes with everything but the egg noodles, use quick release, add the noodles, and cook for an extra 2 minutes.

Carne Mechada

Serves 4 to 6

PREP TIME: **5 MINUTES**

MANUAL/PRESSURE COOK: **5 MINUTES HIGH PRESSURE**

RELEASE: **NATURAL**

TOTAL TIME: **15 MINUTES**

Carne mechada is part of Venezuela's national dish, *pabellón*, which consists of shredded beef, white rice, black beans, and fried ripe plantains. In my house, a *pabellón* was eaten at least once a week. It was one of my abuelito's (grandpa's) signature dishes. I remember waking up at 7 a.m. on school days to find him at the kitchen table shredding the meat. Every country in Latin America has a version of this classic Spanish dish. In Cuba, they call it *ropa vieja* ("old clothes"), a name which, according to Maricel Presilla in her book *Gran Cocina Latina*, refers to the cooking process: "A piece of meat first used to make soup is recycled, pulled into shreds like an old garment, and then braised in a savory sauce."

1. In the pressure-cooker pot, add the beef, sofrito, wine, tomatoes, ketchup, and if using, Worcestershire sauce and cumin. Close and lock the lid.

2. Select the Manual/Pressure Cook setting and cook for 5 minutes at high pressure. When cooking is complete, allow the pressure to release naturally. Carefully unlock and remove the lid. Season with salt and pepper. Serve.

4 cups Shredded Beef (page 96)

1½ cups Sofrito Base Sauce (page 140)

¼ cup red wine

1 cup diced San Marzano tomatoes and juices (canned)

2 tablespoons ketchup

1 tablespoon Worcestershire sauce (optional)

½ teaspoon ground cumin (optional)

Salt

Freshly ground black pepper

OPTION: You can always add more sofrito for a runnier stew consistency. Additionally, to add even more flavor to your beef, season it with some Goya adobo completo before putting it in the pot.

Vaca Frita

Serves 4 to 6

PREP TIME. **25 MINUTES**

SAUTÉ: **15 MINUTES**

TOTAL TIME: **40 MINUTES**

Vaca Frita is a classic Cuban dish which, after being pressure cooked and shredded, is sautéed in a hot skillet (or with the Sauté function in the electric pressure cooker) with a tangy, garlicky Cuban Mojo Sauce (page 143). The shredded meat soaks up the delectable sauce and the edges get nice and crispy. You can have it with rice, inside a tortilla with some pico de gallo, or with guacamole on top—its a very versatile, delicious dish.

1. In a large bowl, combine the meat and mojo sauce and season with salt and pepper. Let it marinate for at least 20 minutes, or cover and leave it in the fridge to marinate overnight.

2. Select the Sauté setting on low and add 2 tablespoons of the olive oil. Once hot, sauté the onions until translucent, about 4 or 5 minutes. Set aside in a large bowl.

3. Select the the Sauté setting on high, and add 2 tablespoons of the olive oil. Once hot, add the beef in batches in a thin even layer, and cook (turning once or twice) about 3 to 5 minutes per batch, or until the beef is sizzling and crispy in spots.

4. Add the cooked beef to the bowl of onions and stir to combine. Drizzle with additional mojo sauce (if desired) and serve.

4 cups Shredded Beef (page 96)

2 cups Cuban Mojo Sauce (page 143), plus additional for serving (optional)

Sea salt

Fresh pepper

4 tablespoons olive oil, divided

1 large onion, thinly sliced

TECHNIQUE: Before browning the beef, take it out of the refrigerator and let it sit at room temperature for at least 20 minutes.

Skirt Steak

Serves 4 to 6

PREP TIME: **5 MINUTES, PLUS 1 TO 5 HOURS MARINATING TIME**
MANUAL/PRESSURE COOK: **4 TO 6 MINUTES LOW PRESSURE**
RELEASE: **QUICK**
TOTAL TIME: **15 MINUTES, PLUS MARINATING TIME**

Skirt steak is an especially flavorful cut of beef and, when cooked properly, is also beautifully tender. This skirt steak, pressure-cooked in beer and adobo seasoning, makes a perfect fajita filling, salad topping, or entrée alongside Potatoes with Chimichurri (page 51).

1. In a resealable bag, combine the beer, Worcestershire sauce, soy sauce, and adobo. Seal and swish around a few times to combine the marinade ingredients.

2. Add the skirt steak and seal the bag. Transfer to the refrigerator and marinate for at least 1 hour or up to 5 hours.

3. In the pressure-cooker pot, add the meat and the marinade.

4. Select the Manual/Pressure Cook setting and cook for 4 minutes at low pressure (for a medium steak) or 6 minutes at low pressure (for a well-done steak). When cooking is complete, quick release the pressure. Carefully unlock and remove the lid.

5. Transfer the meat to a cutting board, and let rest at least 5 minutes before slicing against the grain. Serve.

1 cup **beer**
¼ cup **Worcestershire sauce**
¼ cup **low-sodium soy sauce or tamari**
1 tablespoon **Goya adobo seasoning, or your favorite all-purpose seasoning**
2 pounds **skirt steak**

OPTION: This dish can also be at the center of the table at your next taco party. Just heat up some corn tortillas and add some Herby Queso Fresco (page 36) and pico de gallo (chopped tomatoes, onion, cilantro, and lime). It's a major crowd-pleaser!

Shredded Pork

Serves 6 to 8

PREP TIME: **5 MINUTES**

MANUAL/PRESSURE COOK: **45 MINUTES HIGH PRESSURE**

RELEASE: **NATURAL FOR 10 MINUTES, THEN QUICK**

TOTAL TIME: **1 HOUR 20 MINUTES**

It might seem odd at first to cook pork in evaporated milk, but once you try it, you'll never want to cook it any other way. The milk tenderizes the meat and enhances the sweetness of the orange juice, cinnamon, and cloves. This recipe makes a large batch that will serve as the basis for several meals—just store it in an airtight container in the refrigerator or freezer for later use.

1. Season the pork with salt and put it in the pressure-cooker pot. Squeeze the orange's juice into the pot, then add the orange halves as well. Add the evaporated milk, cinnamon sticks, cloves, bay leaves, and ¼ cup water. Close and lock the lid.

2. Select the Manual/Pressure Cook setting and cook for 45 minutes at high pressure. When cooking is complete, allow the pressure to release naturally for 10 minutes, then quick release any remaining pressure. Carefully unlock and remove the lid.

3. Transfer the pressure-cooker pot to a heatproof surface. Don't worry about the curdled milk—it's normal and imparts lots of flavor! Transfer the pork to a large bowl.

4. Using two forks, shred the meat. Serve right away (see the suggestions at right) or store the meat in an airtight container in the refrigerator for up to 4 days or in the freezer for up to 1 month.

3 pounds boneless pork shoulder, trimmed of excess fat, halved against the grain

Salt

1 orange, halved

1½ cups evaporated milk

2 cinnamon sticks

10 whole cloves

2 bay leaves

ADDITIONAL TIP: The meat is delicious as is, but if you want to take it to the next level, try these quick ways to elevate the meat even further.

FOR CARNITAS: Strain the cooking liquid through a fine strainer or cheesecloth into a medium bowl. Use a ladle to transfer the oil that floats to the top to a small bowl. Set the pressure cooker to Sauté and add about 1 tablespoon of the reserved oil to the pressure-cooker pot. Once the oil is hot, add the pulled pork in batches. Stir occasionally, until the meat is crisp and light golden brown. If you prefer a crispier meat, sauté it in a hot cast-iron skillet instead. Season to taste.

FOR CUBAN: Add Cuban Mojo Sauce (page 143). Serve with rice, beans, yuca, and plantains.

FOR BARBECUE: Add your favorite barbecue sauce. Serve in barbecue pulled-pork sandwiches, over nachos, or with pinto beans.

Bolognese Sauce

Serves 4 to 6

PREP TIME: **10 MINUTES**

SAUTÉ: **10 MINUTES**

MANUAL/PRESSURE COOK: **10 MINUTES**

RELEASE: **NATURAL FOR 10 MINUTES, THEN QUICK**

TOTAL TIME: **50 MINUTES**

A good bolognese sauce is one of my favorite dishes in the world. The vegetables are optional, but they add lots of deep flavor to the sauce for a great way to get in your veggies while still relishing an intensely meaty sauce. I love cooking pasta in the pressure cooker, and this sauce is one of my favorites if you want a true one-pot experience.

1. In a mixing bowl, season the ground beef with salt and pepper. Add the minced garlic and fold in until incorporated. Add the adobo seasoning and mix well.

2. Select the Sauté setting to preheat the pressure-cooker pot.

3. Heat the oil and add the onion, cooking until translucent, about 2 minutes. Add the celery and carrot (if using), and cook until they begin to soften, about 1 to 2 minutes. Add the tomato paste and cook until fragrant, about 1 minute. Deglaze the pot with red wine, scraping the bottom of the pan to dissolve any browned bits.

4. Add the beef and cook until browned, 3 to 5 minutes. Stir in the marinara sauce and season with salt and pepper. Close and lock the lid.

5. Select the Manual/Pressure Cook setting and cook for 10 minutes at high pressure. When cooking is complete, allow the pressure to release naturally for 10 minutes, then quickly release any remaining pressure. Carefully unlock and remove the lid.

6. Serve over your favorite pasta and, if desired, garnish with chopped fresh parsley and grated Parmesan.

1½ pounds ground beef

Salt

Freshly ground black pepper

4 garlic cloves, minced

1 teaspoon Goya adobo seasoning

2 tablespoons extra-virgin olive oil

1 medium white onion, diced

1 large celery stalk, diced (optional)

1 medium carrot, diced (optional)

2 tablespoons tomato paste

1 cup red wine

3½ cups Marinara Sauce (page 139) or 1 (28-ounce) jar marinara sauce

Cooked pasta, for serving

Fresh parsley, chopped, for garnish (optional)

Fresh Parmesan, grated, for garnish (optional)

TECHNIQUE: If you want, you can cook the pasta in with the sauce, but you might need to play with the cook time depending on the type of pasta you're using. You can cook fusilli or other corkscrew pasta right in this delicious sauce in about 6 minutes on high pressure with an added ¼ cup of stock. Use quick release when cooking is complete.

Beef and Broccoli

Serves 4

PREP TIME: **10 MINUTES**

STEAM: **1 MINUTE**

MANUAL/PRESSURE COOK: **12 MINUTES HIGH PRESSURE**

RELEASE: **QUICK**

TOTAL TIME: **30 MINUTES**

This is a quick, easy, and healthy version of the Chinese-takeout favorite. The meat gets lusciously tender and really soaks up all of the flavors of the marinade and other seasonings. All you need to round out this meal is a bowl of steamed rice.

1. In the pressure-cooker pot, add 1 cup water. Place a steamer basket inside the pot and add the broccoli florets. Close and lock the lid.

2. Select the Steam setting for 1 minute. When cooking is complete, quick release the pressure. Unlock and carefully remove the lid. Use tongs to transfer the broccoli to a plate, and remove the steamer basket. Pour out the water from the pressure-cooker pot, wipe the pot dry, and return it to the cooker.

3. Season the steak with salt and pepper.

4. In the pressure-cooker pot, heat 2 tablespoons of sesame oil on the Sauté setting. When the oil is hot, brown the meat, working in batches to avoid crowding the pot. Transfer the cooked meat to a plate.

5. In the pressure-cooker pot, add the remaining 1 tablespoon of sesame oil and the onion, and stir until coated with oil. Cook for about 2 minutes, until softened. Add the teriyaki marinade, beef stock, and red pepper flakes (if using).

Continued

1 pound broccoli florets

1½ pounds flank steak, sliced into thin strips

Salt

Freshly ground black pepper

3 tablespoons sesame oil, divided

1 small onion, thinly sliced

¾ cup store-bought teriyaki marinade sauce

½ cup beef stock (see Shredded Beef, page 96) or water

Pinch red pepper flakes (optional)

2 tablespoons cornstarch

Steamed rice, for serving

TECHNIQUE: Don't cook the broccoli with the beef. I've tried it, and the broccoli basically just disintegrates inside the sauce. That's why I cook the broccoli for a minute first and then just fold it in at the end. Alternatively, you can steam your broccoli for 2 to 3 minutes in the microwave and skip the step of cooking the broccoli in the pressure cooker altogether.

Beef and Broccoli *Continued*

6. Add the beef back into the pot, along with any juices on the plate. Close and lock the lid.

7. Select the Manual/Pressure Cook setting and cook for 12 minutes at high pressure. When cooking is complete, quick release the pressure. Carefully unlock and remove the lid.

8. In a small bowl, whisk together 2 tablespoons water and the cornstarch to make a slurry. Add the slurry to the pressure-cooker pot, and stir. Select Sauté and stir until the sauce comes to a boil and thickens, about 2 minutes. Add in the broccoli and mix well. Serve over rice.

Balsamic-Glazed Pork

Serves 4

PREP TIME: 8 MINUTES
SAUTÉ: **13 MINUTES**
MANUAL/PRESSURE COOK: **2 MINUTES HIGH PRESSURE**
RELEASE: **QUICK**
TOTAL TIME: **30 MINUTES**

This is a showstopper dish that's perfect for a dinner party. You'll be amazed at how a handful of ingredients can make such a beautiful and flavorful roast—and with so little effort, too! Serve it with mashed potatoes and roasted Brussels sprouts for a super-easy but impressive meal.

4 (6-ounce) bone-in
    pork chops
Salt
Freshly ground black pepper
1 tablespoon extra-virgin
    olive oil, divided
¼ cup balsamic vinegar
3 tablespoons honey
2 tablespoons cornstarch
Fresh thyme, chopped,
    for garnish

INGREDIENT TIP: Try to use a high-quality balsamic vinegar, because that's the base of the dish and all that flavor will go into the finished product. Also, if your pork chops are more than 1½ inches thick, you may want to increase the pressure cooking time by 1 minute.

1. Select the Sauté setting to preheat the pressure-cooker pot.

2. Season the pork chops with salt and pepper. When the pressure-cooker pot is hot, add ½ tablespoon of oil and half the pork chops, browning on each side for 1 minute. Remove and set aside on a plate. Repeat with the remaining ½ tablespoon of oil and pork chops.

3. Place all the pork chops back in the pressure-cooker pot and add ¼ cup water, the balsamic vinegar, and the honey. Close and lock the lid.

4. Select the Manual/Pressure Cook setting and cook for 2 minutes at high pressure. When cooking is complete, quick release the pressure. Carefully unlock and remove the lid. Remove the pork chops and set aside.

5. Adjust to the Sauté function for 3 minutes to reduce the cooking liquid.

6. In a small bowl, combine 3 tablespoons of the cooking liquid and the cornstarch, and whisk to create a slurry. Add the slurry back into the cooking liquid and mix well. Stir until the sauce thickens, 1 to 2 minutes.

7. Pour the sauce over the pork chops, garnish with thyme if desired, and serve.

Korean-Style Short Ribs

Serves 4

PREP TIME: **10 MINUTES, PLUS 1 HOUR TO OVERNIGHT MARINATING TIME**
MANUAL/PRESSURE COOK: **5 MINUTES HIGH PRESSURE**
RELEASE: **QUICK**
TOTAL TIME: **20 MINUTES, PLUS MARINATING TIME**

You'll want to make a large batch of these melt-in-your-mouth ribs because everyone who tries them will be asking for more. Marinating the beef ahead of time intensifies the flavors. You can also put the meat in the marinade and freeze it in resealable plastic bags. Simply thaw before cooking, and you're ready to go.

1. In a resealable plastic bag, combine the Korean barbecue marinade and peanut butter. Marinate the short ribs in the bag for at least 1 hour or as long as overnight (in the refrigerator).

2. In the pressure-cooker pot, arrange the ribs. Pour the beef stock into the marinade bag and swish it around to loosen the remaining marinade. Pour the marinade and stock into the pressure-cooker pot. Close and lock the lid.

3. Select the Manual/Pressure Cook setting and cook for 5 minutes at high pressure. When cooking is complete, quick release the pressure. Carefully unlock and remove the lid.

4. Transfer the ribs to a plate and cut between the bones. To serve, garnish with sliced scallions and sesame seeds.

1 cup Korean barbecue marinade
3 tablespoons creamy peanut butter
2½ pounds thinly sliced flanken beef short ribs
1 cup beef stock (see Shredded Beef, page 96)
3 scallions, sliced, for garnish
Sesame seeds, for garnish

OPTION: After removing the ribs to a plate, set the cooker to Sauté, and let the sauce reduce for about 3 minutes. Pour the sauce over the ribs.

Baby Back Ribs

Serves 4

PREP TIME: **10 MINUTES**

MANUAL/PRESSURE COOK: **25 MINUTES HIGH PRESSURE**

RELEASE: **QUICK**

TOTAL TIME: **45 MINUTES**

Yes, yes, yes! You can have delicious, finger-licking, falling-off-the-bone, barbecue-flavored ribs any time—even if you live in a New York City apartment like I do. A flavorful spice rub and 25 minutes in the pressure cooker tenderizes these ribs and infuses them with that barbecue flavor you love.

1. In a small bowl, combine the salt, paprika, garlic powder, cumin, and pepper. Set aside.

2. Using a sharp knife, remove the thin membrane from the back of the ribs, if desired. Cut the ribs into thirds, so you have easier pieces to manage. Rub the spice mixture onto the ribs, coating well.

3. In the pressure-cooker pot, pour in the beef stock and arrange the ribs upright like a teepee. Close and lock the lid.

4. Select the Manual/Pressure Cook setting and cook for 25 minutes at high pressure. When cooking is complete, quick release the pressure. Carefully unlock and remove the lid. Serve.

2 tablespoons salt

1 tablespoon paprika

2 teaspoons garlic powder

1 teaspoon ground cumin

1 teaspoon freshly ground black pepper

1 (2-pound) baby-back-rib rack

1 cup beef stock (see Shredded Beef, page 96) or water

OPTION: Brush the ribs with your favorite barbecue sauce before serving. I like one with a bit of smoke, maple syrup, and bourbon.

Creamy Mussels

Serves 4

PREP TIME: **10 MINUTES**

MANUAL/PRESSURE COOK: **2 MINUTES HIGH PRESSURE**

RELEASE: **QUICK**

TOTAL TIME: **20 MINUTES**

Fresh shellfish always seems fancy and challenging, but this dish is crazy easy to make. Whole (cleaned) mussels go in the electric pressure cooker along with a bit of wine and mustard. With just 2 minutes of pressure-cooking time, the mussels will pop open their shells and become plump, tender, and ready to devour. Stir in some crème fraîche and garnish with fresh parsley for a professional touch. Be sure to have a loaf of crusty bread to serve on the side—you'll want to soak up every bit of the creamy sauce.

1. Scrub the mussels under cold running water and remove the beards (the bristly material sticking out from one side) by pulling down toward the hinge of the shell and outward. Use a towel for leverage—mussels hold onto their beards fiercely.

2. In the pressure-cooker pot, add the mussels, Dijon mustard, and white wine. Close and lock the lid.

3. Select the Manual/Pressure Cook setting and cook for 2 minutes at high pressure. When cooking is complete, quick release the pressure. Carefully unlock and remove the lid.

4. Transfer the mussels to a serving platter, discarding any that didn't open. Whisk the crème fraîche into the pressure-cooker pot to thicken the juices, then pour the sauce over the mussels. Serve, garnished with parsley and accompanied by crusty bread.

1 pound mussels

½ cup Dijon mustard

¼ cup white wine

¼ cup crème fraîche

¼ cup chopped fresh parsley leaves, for garnish

Crusty bread, for serving

OPTION: For more freshness, squeeze a bit of lemon juice on top of the mussels. You can also substitute the wine for beer, if desired.

Shrimp with Guajillo Chiles

Serves 4

PREP TIME: **15 MINUTES**

MANUAL/PRESSURE COOK: **5 MINUTES HIGH PRESSURE, 2 MINUTES LOW PRESSURE**

RELEASE: **QUICK**

TOTAL TIME: **30 MINUTES, PLUS 1 HOUR 30 MINUTES CHILLING TIME**

Guajillo chiles aren't very spicy—they're actually quite sweet, with deep berry and raisin notes. In this multi-step recipe, you'll make the guajillo marinade, cool it, marinate the shrimp, and then quickly pressure-cook it. It sounds complicated, but each of the steps takes only a couple of minutes, and the resulting dish is so worth it. You can use the leftover marinade with chicken, pork, or beef, as well.

1. In the pressure-cooker pot, combine the guajillo chiles, garlic, oil, orange juice, brown sugar, cumin (if using), and 2 cups of water. Close and lock the lid.

2. Select the Manual/Pressure Cook setting and cook for 5 minutes at high pressure. When cooking is complete, quick release the pressure. Unlock and carefully remove the lid.

3. Using an immersion blender (or transferring the marinade to a regular blender), blend the marinade until completely smooth. Pour 1 cup of the marinade into a resealable bag, and cool in the refrigerator for about 30 minutes. Transfer the remaining marinade to an airtight container and store for up to 1 week in the refrigerator or up to 3 months in the freezer.

Continued

8 dried guajillo chiles, cut lengthwise and seeded

2 garlic cloves, peeled

¼ cup canola oil or other neutral-flavored oil

¼ cup orange juice

2 tablespoons brown sugar

1 teaspoon ground cumin (optional)

2 pounds (about 36) shrimp, peeled and deveined

Salt

INGREDIENT TIP: Buy guajillo chiles online, in Latin markets, or in the ethnic section of some supermarkets. You can serve these shrimp with white or Pesto Rice (page 44), or put them inside a tortilla with some guacamole.

Shrimp with Guajillo Chiles *Continued*

4. Add the shrimp to the marinade, seal the bag, and refrigerate for at least 1 hour or overnight at the maximum.

5. Transfer the shrimp and marinade to the pressure-cooker pot. Select the Manual/Pressure Cook setting and cook for 2 minutes at low pressure. When cooking is complete, quick release the pressure. Carefully unlock and remove the lid. Transfer the shrimp to a serving plate and season with salt. Serve.

Italian-Style Steamed Cod with Escarole

Serves 4

PREP TIME: **5 MINUTES**

SAUTÉ: **5 MINUTES**

MANUAL/PRESSURE COOK: **2 MINUTES LOW PRESSURE**

RELEASE: **QUICK**

TOTAL TIME: **20 MINUTES**

This is a great weeknight meal: quick, easy to make, healthy, and delicious. Even if you don't like anchovies, I urge you to use them in this recipe. They add depth of flavor without tasting strong, fishy, or overly salty. You won't even know there are anchovies in the dish, but you'll love the subtle flavor they add.

1. In the pressure-cooker pot, combine the garlic, anchovy fillets, and olive oil. Select the Sauté setting and cook for 3 minutes, stirring regularly. With a wooden spoon, break the anchovy fillets apart so they disappear into the oil.

2. Add the red pepper flakes, and 30 seconds later, add the escarole. Sauté for 1 minute, stirring throughout. Add ½ cup water and place the cod fillets in the cooker. Season with the salt. Close and lock the lid.

3. Select the Manual/Pressure Cook setting and cook for 2 minutes at low pressure. When cooking is complete, quick release the pressure. Unlock and carefully remove the lid.

4. Using a slotted spoon, transfer the fish fillets to a serving plate and place the escarole on the side. Serve.

2 garlic cloves, sliced

2 anchovy fillets

1 tablespoon extra-virgin olive oil

Pinch red pepper flakes

2 escarole heads, leaves washed and chopped into 1-inch pieces

4 (6-ounce) cod fillets, about 1 inch thick

½ teaspoon salt

OPTION: If you'd like to make a sauce out of the liquid, use the Sauté setting to reduce the liquid to your desired thickness. Also, for a dash of freshness, serve alongside lemon wedges.

Arroz Negro

Serves 4

PREP TIME: **10 MINUTES**

SAUTÉ: **5 MINUTES**

MANUAL/PRESSURE COOK: **6 MINUTES HIGH PRESSURE**

RELEASE: **QUICK**

TOTAL TIME: **30 MINUTES**

If you want to impress people, make this Spanish-style black rice. The flavors are bold, and the squid ink gives it a very dramatic look. It's traditionally prepared on the stove top, but that's time-consuming and requires constant attention. With the electric pressure cooker, you just put the ingredients in the pot and walk away. You can find squid ink at fish markets, specialty grocers, and online. Enjoy the finished dish with a glass of Albariño, and you'll feel like you're dining in Barcelona.

1. Set the electric pressure cooker to the Sauté setting on low heat. In the pressure-cooker pot, add the olive oil, garlic, and parsley, if desired, and cook for about 2 minutes, being careful not to burn the garlic.

2. Add the rice, stirring regularly for about 2 minutes. Deglaze the pot with the wine, scraping up any bits stuck to the bottom of the pot.

3. Add the squid ink and squid (if using), and stir until all the rice is coated with the ink. Pour in the sofrito and fish stock. Season with salt. Close and lock the lid.

4. Select the Manual/Pressure Cook setting and cook for 6 minutes at high pressure. When cooking is complete, quick release the pressure. Unlock and carefully remove the lid.

5. Season with salt and chopped fresh parsley (if using). Serve immediately.

2 tablespoons extra-virgin olive oil

4 garlic cloves, minced

¼ cup chopped fresh parsley (optional)

1 cup arborio rice

¼ cup white wine

2 tablespoons black squid ink

¼ pound squid, chopped (optional)

1 cup Sofrito Base Sauce (page 140)

1 cup Fish Stock (page 135) or water

Salt

Fresh parsley leaves, chopped, for garnish (optional)

TROUBLESHOOTING: When cooking is finished, open the pressure cooker and stir to combine. If the rice is too soupy, turn on the Sauté function and stir until the desired consistency is achieved. You can add a drizzle of high-quality olive oil at this time as well. If the rice is too thick, add some wine and stir. If you don't have stock, you can use water with a pinch or two of salt. If you happen to make the Spanish-Style Octopus (page 114) before this recipe, you can use the stock from that in place of the fish stock, as it will impart a great flavor.

Salmon with Lemon and Parsley

Serves 4

PREP TIME: **5 MINUTES**

MANUAL/PRESSURE COOK: **1 MINUTE LOW PRESSURE**

RELEASE: **QUICK**

TOTAL TIME: **20 MINUTES**

This is another favorite weeknight meal for me because it's quick to make, healthy, and delicious. Cooking fish wrapped in parchment or foil is great, because it infuses the flavors into the fish, rather than letting them be watered down as they would be if you steamed the fish without the wrapping. The wrapping also makes cleanup a breeze. Be sure to use the low pressure setting on your electric pressure cooker, since salmon can overcook quickly.

1. In the pressure-cooker pot, add 1 cup of water and place the trivet inside.

2. Lay the salmon fillet in the center of a large piece of aluminum foil or parchment.

3. Pour the wine and coconut oil over the fish. Season with salt and pepper.

4. Lay the lemon slices neatly on top of the fish, and place the reserved parsley stems on both sides of the fish. Fold up the foil or parchment like a packet to seal in the fish. Place the packet on top of the trivet. Close and lock the lid.

5. Select the Manual/Pressure Cook setting and cook for 1 minute at low pressure. When cooking is complete, quick release the pressure. Unlock and carefully remove the lid.

6. Remove the packet and carefully open it. Discard the parsley stems. Transfer the salmon to a plate and garnish with the freshly chopped parsley leaves. Serve immediately.

1 (20-ounce) salmon fillet

¼ cup white wine

1½ tablespoons coconut oil, melted

Salt

Freshly ground black pepper

1 lemon, sliced into ¼-inch rounds

Few parsley sprigs, leaves chopped and stems reserved

OPTION: I use fresh fish, but if you want to use frozen, you can. Just leave it in the electric pressure cooker for 5 minutes instead of 1 minute. If you want to make this into a full meal, you can add 1 cup of long-grain rice, 2 cups of water, some salt, and a squirt of oil at the bottom of the pot. Place the trivet with the wrapped fish on it inside the pot, and there you have it—a complete meal in a few minutes.

Spanish-Style Octopus

Serves 4

PREP TIME: **5 MINUTES**

SAUTÉ: **1 MINUTE**

MANUAL/PRESSURE COOK: **15 MINUTES HIGH PRESSURE**

RELEASE: **QUICK**

TOTAL TIME: **30 MINUTES**

Octopus may seem intimidating, but rest assured, the electric pressure cooker is the ideal way to cook it. You only need to add a small amount of water, since the octopus will release a good amount of liquid. In fact, that liquid will become a flavorful stock that you can use to make a fabulous Shrimp Chupe (page 64) or Arroz Negro (page 112).

1. Set the pressure cooker to the Sauté function. Add the olive oil and garlic, and sauté for about 1 minute. Add the octopus, ¼ cup water, and bay leaves. Close and lock the lid.

2. Select the Manual/Pressure Cook setting and cook for 15 minutes at high pressure. When cooking is complete, quick release the pressure. Unlock and carefully remove the lid.

3. Wait for the octopus to cool down a bit, then cut it with scissors into bite-size pieces. Drizzle with olive oil, and garnish with paprika and salt. Serve immediately.

3 tablespoons extra-virgin olive oil

3 garlic cloves, peeled and smashed

2 pounds frozen octopus, thawed

2 bay leaves

Drizzle extra-virgin olive oil, for serving

1 teaspoon smoked Spanish paprika, for serving

Pinch flaky sea salt, for serving

INGREDIENT TIP: Frozen octopus is best, because the meat actually gets more tender when it's frozen.

Mushroom Risotto

Serves 4

PREP TIME: **10 MINUTES**

SAUTÉ: **14 MINUTES**

MANUAL/PRESSURE COOK: **6 MINUTES HIGH PRESSURE**

RELEASE: **QUICK**

TOTAL TIME: **35 MINUTES**

I was skeptical that the electric pressure cooker could make a decent risotto, but the results amazed me! No more standing over the stove for 45 minutes. The key is to stir in cold butter just before serving to give it the creaminess you expect from a good risotto.

1. Select the Sauté setting to preheat the pressure-cooker pot.

2. When hot, add the olive oil and 1 tablespoon of butter. Add the onion and a bit of salt to help release moisture so you don't brown the onions. Cook until translucent, about 2 minutes.

3. Add the mushrooms and garlic (if using). Season with salt to help them release moisture, and cook for about 7 minutes. Place the lid on top for about 1 minute so that the mushrooms release some liquid and get soft quickly without burning.

4. Add the rice, and stir for about 2 minutes. Deglaze with the wine, scraping up any bits from the bottom of the pot, then let reduce by half until you can no longer smell the alcohol, about 2 minutes.

5. Pour in the vegetable stock or water and mix well. Close and lock the lid.

6. Select the Manual/Pressure Cook setting and cook for 6 minutes at high pressure. When cooking is complete, quick release the pressure. Unlock and carefully remove the lid. Stir in the remaining 2 tablespoons of cold cubed butter and the grated Parmesan. Season with pepper and chopped fresh parsley (if using), and top with more grated Parmesan (if desired). Serve immediately.

1 tablespoon extra-virgin olive oil

3 tablespoons cold butter, cut into 6 cubes, divided

¾ cup finely diced onion or shallot (about 1 small onion or 2 shallots)

Salt

2 cups sliced mixed mushrooms (baby bella, shiitake, and oyster)

1 garlic clove, minced (optional)

1 cup arborio rice

¼ cup white wine

2 cups Vegetable Stock (page 136) or water

½ cup grated Parmesan, plus more for garnish (optional)

Freshly ground black pepper

Chopped fresh parsley (optional)

TROUBLESHOOTING: Once you open the lid, if the risotto is too thick for your liking, stir in some hot stock or water. If it's too thin, turn on the Sauté function for a few minutes and stir until it reaches the desired consistency. Remember, adding butter and Parmesan will help thicken it and make it creamy.

SUBSTITUTION: You can use Chicken Stock (page 134) instead of vegetable stock, but then the dish won't be vegetarian.

Edamame Fried Rice

Serves 4

PREP TIME: **10 MINUTES**

SAUTÉ: **5 MINUTES**

RICE OR MANUAL/PRESSURE COOK: **8 MINUTES HIGH PRESSURE**

RELEASE: **NATURAL FOR 10 MINUTES, THEN QUICK**

KEEP WARM: **1 MINUTE**

TOTAL TIME: **40 MINUTES**

This vegetarian version of a takeout favorite is packed with protein. If you want to add more vegetables, add frozen (thawed) peas and carrots along with the edamame and/or diced tomato after folding in the egg. If you want to add meat, diced Chinese sausage or ham works well. Brown the meat in the pressure-cooker pot first, transfer to a plate, and then add it back to the pot at the end of cooking.

1. Select the Sauté setting to preheat the pressure-cooker pot.

2. When hot, add 1 tablespoon of sesame oil and the onion. Cook for about 3 minutes. Add the rice and vegetable stock. Close and lock the lid.

3. Select the Rice or Manual/Pressure Cook setting and cook for 8 minutes at high pressure. When cooking is complete, allow the pressure to release naturally for 10 minutes, then quick release any remaining pressure. Unlock and carefully remove the lid.

4. Stir in the edamame. Close and lock the lid, and select 1 minute on the Keep Warm setting with the vent closed. Then remove the lid.

5. Using a spatula, push the rice and edamame to the edges, to create a well in the center of the pot. Adjust the pressure cooker to the Sauté setting. Add the remaining 1 table-spoon of sesame oil, and pour in the beaten eggs. Season with a little salt, and start scrambling the eggs. When nearly scrambled, after about 45 seconds, fold in the rice and edamame, and stir gently to combine.

6. Turn off the cooker, add the soy sauce, and mix well. Serve, garnished with scallion (if using).

Ingredients

2 tablespoons sesame oil, divided

1 small onion, finely diced (about ½ cup)

1 cup jasmine rice

1¼ cups Vegetable Stock (page 136) or water

1 cup frozen shelled edamame, thawed

2 large eggs, beaten

Salt

3 tablespoons soy sauce

Scallion, thinly sliced (optional)

INGREDIENT TIP: Edamame are immature soybeans, and they make a great addition to vegetarian dishes. They look similar to oversize peas when in their pods, and are commonly sold, shelled or unshelled, in the freezer section at most well-stocked grocery stores.

Easy Mac and Cheese

Serves 8

PREP TIME: **5 MINUTES**

MANUAL/PRESSURE COOK: **2 MINUTES HIGH PRESSURE**

RELEASE: **QUICK**

TOTAL TIME: **15 MINUTES**

Electric-pressure-cooker mac and cheese is a dream come true. It takes only 15 minutes to make from start to finish—honestly not that much longer than the stuff that comes in a box—and it is pure, creamy, rich comfort in a bowl. I like to top mine with grated Parmesan and chili flakes to take it up a notch.

1. In the pressure-cooker pot, add the macaroni, butter, salt, and 4 cups water. Close and lock the lid.

2. Select the Manual/Pressure Cook setting and cook for 2 minutes at high pressure. When cooking is complete, quick release the pressure. Unlock and carefully remove the lid.

3. Adjust the pressure cooker to the Sauté setting. Add the cream or milk, ¼ cup at a time, until the desired consistency is achieved.

4. Add the shredded cheese and the nutmeg and cayenne (if using). Season with salt to taste. Remove the pot from the cooker, and serve immediately.

1 (16-ounce) box elbow macaroni

3 tablespoons butter

1 tablespoon salt, plus more for seasoning

1 cup heavy cream or whole milk

2 cups shredded Cheddar cheese

Pinch nutmeg (optional)

Pinch ground cayenne pepper (optional)

TROUBLESHOOTING: Make sure you add enough salt to your water! That's the trick to making good pasta or rice that isn't bland. It should be about as salty as the ocean.

Fruity Cheesecake with Chocolate Cookie Crust, *page 125*

CHAPTER 7

Desserts

You might not think the electric pressure cooker would be great at turning out desserts, and yet, it is! Of course, it's perfect for steeping festive beverages like Mexican Hot Chocolate (page 128) and Mulled Wine (page 129), but it also makes delightful cakes, cheesecakes, puddings, and cooked fruits.

Steel-Cut Oatcake

Serves 4 to 6

PREP TIME: **10 MINUTES**

MANUAL/PRESSURE COOK: **25 MINUTES HIGH PRESSURE**

RELEASE: **NATURAL FOR 10 MINUTES, THEN QUICK**

TOTAL TIME: **1 HOUR**

This cake is almost like a chewy granola bar. It makes a nice not-too-sweet dessert or a healthy snack. The key ingredient, chai concentrate, is just what it sounds like: the spices and herbs used in chai tea (cinnamon, cloves, cardamom, etc.), steeped for a long time in hot water. It's available in many supermarkets, but if you can't find it there, you can order it online or simply substitute vanilla extract and a dash of pumpkin pie spice.

1½ teaspoons butter

2 cups whole milk

¼ cup honey

Pinch salt

2 teaspoons chai concentrate (or ½ teaspoon vanilla extract and a dash of pumpkin pie spice)

1 cup steel-cut oats

¼ cup raisins or diced dried fruit medley

SUBSTITUTION: If you want to make this recipe dairy-free, use 1¾ cups almond milk in place of the 2 cups whole milk.

1. Coat the inside of a 7-inch baking dish with the butter.

2. In the pressure-cooker pot, add 1 cup water and place the trivet inside.

3. In a mixing bowl, whisk together the milk, honey, salt, and chai concentrate (or vanilla extract and pumpkin pie spice) until very well combined. Add in the oats and raisins or dried fruit medley, and whisk until just combined.

4. Pour the oat mixture into the prepared baking dish. Cover with foil and place on the trivet. Close and lock the lid.

5. Select the Manual/Pressure Cook setting and cook for 25 minutes at high pressure. When cooking is complete, allow the pressure to release naturally for 10 minutes, then quick release any remaining pressure. Unlock and carefully open the lid.

6. Remove the baking dish and let sit for 5 minutes before removing the foil. Invert the cake onto a plate and cut into wedges before serving.

Red-Wine-Poached Pears

Serves 4 to 8

PREP TIME: **5 MINUTES**

MANUAL/PRESSURE COOK: **8 MINUTES HIGH PRESSURE**

RELEASE: **QUICK**

TOTAL TIME: **20 MINUTES**

- 1 (750-milliliter) bottle red wine
- ½ cup brown sugar
- 3 whole cloves
- 1 lemon, zested and cut in half
- 4 whole pears, peeled
- Vanilla ice cream, for serving (optional)
- Toasted coconut, for serving (optional)
- Mint leaves, for garnish (optional)

OPTION: Set the cooker to Sauté and reduce the liquid by half or until it reaches a syrupy consistency, about 10 minutes. Remove the lemon, and spoon the sauce over the pears. Enjoy!

Just looking at these beauties makes me smile, especially because I know they taste as good as they look. They make an elegant ending for a dinner party and are especially welcome when you want something lighter than the usual sugar- and fat-heavy dessert options. Of course, they're best served with a scoop of vanilla ice cream on the side. Add a sprinkle of toasted coconut on top, and you have yourself a guaranteed showstopper.

1. In the pressure-cooker pot, add the wine, brown sugar, cloves, lemon halves, and lemon zest. Stir until the sugar is dissolved.

2. Place the pears in the poaching liquid, and spoon some of the liquid over the tops of the pears. Close and lock the lid.

3. Select the Manual/Pressure Cook setting and cook for 8 minutes at high pressure. When cooking is complete, quick release the pressure. Unlock and carefully remove the lid. Using a slotted spoon, transfer the pears to serving dishes. If using, serve with vanilla ice cream and toasted coconut or mint leaves.

Pineapple-Coconut Tapioca Pudding

Serves 4 to 6

PREP TIME: **5 MINUTES**

MANUAL/PRESSURE COOK: **15 MINUTES HIGH PRESSURE**

RELEASE: **QUICK**

TOTAL TIME: **30 MINUTES**

1 (20-ounce) can crushed pineapple

1¼ cups coconut milk

⅓ cup tapioca pearls, rinsed

¼ cup sugar

Pinch salt

¼ cup sweetened toasted coconut flakes (optional)

Tapioca is the starch extracted from the cassava root, and it's a common ingredient in Latin American cuisines. With its mild taste, tapioca makes a great starchy base for all sorts of sweet flavors. Of course, it's particularly well suited to tropical flavors like coconut and fresh pineapple. This dessert is also naturally gluten-free, making it a good choice when you're serving people who are sensitive to gluten.

INGREDIENT TIP: Tapioca is a traditional Brazilian food that was once widely used as a thickener and in puddings in the United States before gelatin became a mainstay. If it's not in your regular supermarket, you can find it at specialty grocers, as well as in Latin and Asian markets.

1. In the pressure-cooker pot, add 1 cup of water and place the trivet inside.

2. In a 7-inch baking dish, mix the crushed pineapple, coconut milk, tapioca pearls, ½ cup water, sugar, and salt. Mix well, and cover with foil. Lower onto the trivet. Close and lock the lid.

3. Select the Manual/Pressure Cook setting and cook for 15 minutes at high pressure. When cooking is complete, quick release the pressure. Carefully unlock and remove the lid, then carefully remove the pan and foil.

4. Top with the coconut flakes (if using) and serve.

Chocolate Chip Chickpea Pudding

Serves 8 to 10

PREP TIME: **10 MINUTES**

MANUAL/PRESSURE COOK: **25 MINUTES HIGH PRESSURE**

RELEASE: **NATURAL**

TOTAL TIME: **1 HOUR**

1 (19-ounce) can chickpeas, drained and rinsed

1 large egg

½ cup creamy peanut butter

⅓ cup honey

¼ cup semisweet chocolate chips

¼ cup pitted, diced dates (optional)

SUBSTITUTE: Make it vegan by using vegan chocolate chips and swapping out the honey for maple syrup or sugar. Replace the egg with a "flax egg" by adding 1 tablespoon of ground flaxseed to 3 tablespoons of water, mixing, and letting sit for 15 minutes to thicken.

I love chocolate, but I don't like to load up on a ton of refined sugar and other empty-calorie foods. This luscious chocolate chip pudding is the perfect solution. It's so creamy and chocolaty that you'll feel like you're eating a decadent treat. You'd never guess that it's made from beans! The sweetness comes from a bit of honey, chocolate chips, and, if you want, dates. If desired, cook the pudding in small ramekins for individual serving sizes.

1. In the pressure-cooker pot, add 1 cup of water and place the trivet inside.

2. Cut a piece of parchment paper to fit a 7-inch baking dish, large enough to extend about 2 inches over the edges of the dish. Place the parchment in the dish and set aside.

3. In a food processor, combine the chickpeas, egg, peanut butter, and honey. Blend until smooth.

4. Pour the mixture into the prepared pan and sprinkle with the chocolate chips and the dates (if using). Cover with aluminum foil and place on the steam rack. Close and lock the lid.

5. Select the Manual/Pressure Cook setting and cook for 25 minutes at high pressure. When cooking is complete, allow the pressure to release naturally. Carefully unlock and remove the lid.

6. Carefully lift the pan from the cooker and remove the foil. Lift the pudding out using the parchment, and place it on a serving plate.

7. Let the pudding cool for a few minutes; it will thicken as it sits. Serve warm or cold.

Matcha Crème Brûlée

Serves 6

PREP TIME: **5 MINUTES**

MANUAL/PRESSURE COOK: **5 MINUTES HIGH PRESSURE**

RELEASE: **NATURAL FOR 10 MINUTES, THEN QUICK**

TOTAL TIME: **30 MINUTES, PLUS 1 TO 2 HOURS CHILLING TIME**

Matcha—the super-trendy, bright-green ingredient you've seen popping up in everything from morning lattes to wedding cakes—is finely ground green tea. It has all the health benefits of green tea: antioxidants, phytochemicals, and amino acids that pep you up, improve your focus, and even reduce your risk of cancer. It's a great way to turn an indulgent dessert like crème brûlée into something you can call "healthy" without going too far out on a limb. I love the delicate yet exotic flavor it adds to the rich, sweet cream custard.

1. In a medium bowl, beat together the egg yolks, sugar, matcha, and vanilla until well combined. Fold in the heavy cream until just mixed together, about 1 minute. Fill six small (1- to 1½-cup) ramekins with ½ cup of filling each. Cover each with foil.

2. In the pressure-cooker pot, add 1 cup of water and place the trivet inside. Place two ramekins side by side, and stack the others on top of them. Close and lock the lid.

3. Select the Manual/Pressure Cook setting and cook for 5 minutes at high pressure. When cooking is complete, allow the pressure to release naturally for 10 minutes, then quick release any remaining pressure. Unlock and carefully remove the lid.

4. Carefully remove the ramekins and chill for 1 to 2 hours.

5. When ready to serve, sprinkle additional sugar evenly over the tops and torch until light brown or set the oven to broil and place the ramekins on the oven rack positioned on the second highest tier. Serve.

8 egg yolks

⅓ cup sugar, plus more for torching

1 tablespoon matcha powder

1 teaspoon vanilla extract

2 cups heavy cream

TECHNIQUE: I like to first whisk the matcha with a teaspoon of heavy cream using a bamboo matcha whisk until well combined. Then I add the mixture to the rest of the ingredients and proceed as usual. This prevents the finely ground matcha from forming any clumps.

Fruity Cheesecake with Chocolate Cookie Crust

Serves 6 to 8

PREP TIME: **10 MINUTES**

MANUAL/PRESSURE COOK: **25 MINUTES HIGH PRESSURE**

RELEASE: **NATURAL FOR 10 MINUTES, THEN QUICK**

TOTAL TIME: **55 MINUTES, PLUS 3 TO 4 HOURS CHILLING TIME**

Who would have thought you could make cheesecake in a pressure cooker? This gorgeous and tasty dessert proves that you absolutely can. You can even achieve a crunchy crust for that most desired textural contrast. And all it takes is four simple ingredients! I love this dessert not just because it's simple to make in the electric pressure cooker, but also because it's delicious and beautiful to boot. Just be careful, because you won't be able to stop eating this dessert until it's gone.

1. In the bowl of a food processor, add the cookies and blend to a sand-like consistency.

2. Spray a 7-inch springform pan with cooking spray, and press the cookie crumbs into the bottom of the pan to form a crust.

3. In a medium bowl, combine the reserved cookie filling, cream cheese, and egg. Mix until well combined.

4. Pour the mixture into the prepared pan and spread evenly. Add the fruit spread in dollops and, using a knife or chopstick, swirl to make a design. Cover with aluminum foil.

5. In the pressure-cooker pot, add 1 cup of water and place the trivet inside it. Carefully place the cheesecake on the trivet. Close and lock the lid.

Continued

10 Oreo cookies, filling removed and reserved

Cooking spray

8 ounces cream cheese

1 large egg

2 tablespoons raspberry or pomegranate spread

Fresh raspberries or pomegranate seeds, for garnish

SUBSTITUTION: If you don't have raspberry or pomegranate spread, other fruit spreads like strawberry, blackberry, and blueberry will work great here as well.

Fruity Cheesecake with Chocolate Cookie Crust *Continued*

6. Select the Manual/Pressure Cook setting and cook for 25 minutes on high pressure. When cooking is complete, allow the pressure to release naturally for 10 minutes, then quick release any remaining pressure. Carefully unlock and remove the lid.

7. Remove the pan from the cooker and let the cheesecake cool at room temperature for 15 minutes. Transfer to the refrigerator and chill for 3 to 4 hours. Serve, garnished with fresh raspberries or pomegranate seeds.

Dulce de Leche

Serves 4

PREP TIME: **1 MINUTE**

MANUAL/PRESSURE COOK: **40 MINUTES HIGH PRESSURE**

RELEASE: **NATURAL**

TOTAL TIME: **55 MINUTES**

Once you try this easy pressure cooker dulce de leche recipe, you'll never buy another jar of the dreamy caramel spread again. This recipe has only one ingredient—sweetened condensed milk—so virtually no prep is needed. You just put the open can, covered with foil, in the electric pressure cooker, set it for 40 minutes, and let the pressure release naturally after the cooking time ends. You'll end up with a treat so intensely delicious that you'll want to eat it straight from the can with a spoon. I like to spread it on toast or use it as filling for the Latin sandwich cookies called *alfajores*.

1. Remove the paper label from the can of condensed milk and discard it. Open the can and discard the top. Cover the can with aluminum foil.

2. Place the trivet in the pressure-cooker pot and place the can of condensed milk on the rack.

3. Add enough water to the pressure-cooker pot to reach halfway up the sides of the can. Close and lock the lid.

4. Select the Manual/Pressure Cook setting and cook for 40 minutes at high pressure. When cooking is complete, allow the pressure to release naturally. Carefully unlock and remove the lid.

5. Carefully remove the can and let it rest on a heatproof surface. Remove the foil and let it cool. Use the dulce de leche immediately, or transfer to an airtight container and store, refrigerated, for up to 3 weeks.

1 (14-ounce) can sweetened condensed milk

TROUBLESHOOTING: Be sure that you securely cover the can with foil. If the foil is loosely placed, the condensed milk might splatter all over when cooking, which will leave you with a mess to clean up and less dulce de leche to enjoy.

Mexican Hot Chocolate

Serves 4 to 6

PREP TIME: **5 MINUTES**
MANUAL/PRESSURE COOK: **2 MINUTES HIGH PRESSURE**
RELEASE: **NATURAL**
TOTAL TIME: **25 MINUTES**

4 ounces bittersweet chocolate
4 cups whole milk
½ cup sweetened condensed milk
½ teaspoon ground cinnamon
Pinch cayenne pepper
Pinch nutmeg (optional)

INGREDIENT TIP: Using a high-quality bittersweet chocolate will yield the richest chocolaty flavor in this comforting drink. Look for a chocolate that contains 35 to 50 percent chocolate liquor and up to 15 percent cocoa butter.

Like any good hot chocolate, this one starts with milk and a high-quality bittersweet chocolate, but the sweetened condensed milk, cinnamon, and cayenne in this version really take it over the top. When I was growing up, Día de los Muertos in late autumn marked the beginning of hot-chocolate season, when the air would be filled with the enticing aroma of chocolate and spices. We used a carved wooden tool called a *molinillo* to whisk the hot chocolate and make it frothy just before serving. If you don't have a *molinillo*, you can use a whisk for a similar effect.

1. In the pressure-cooker pot, combine the chocolate, whole milk, condensed milk, ½ cup water, cinnamon, cayenne, and nutmeg (if using). Close and lock the lid.

2. Select the Manual/Pressure Cook setting and cook for 2 minutes at high pressure. When cooking is complete, allow the pressure to release naturally for 15 minutes. Unlock and carefully remove the lid.

3. Using a wire mesh strainer set over a bowl, strain the hot chocolate to remove any solids, then return the strained liquid to the pressure-cooker pot. Using an immersion blender or whisk, blend to create froth. Serve.

Mulled Wine

Serves 5 or 6

PREP TIME: **5 MINUTES**

MANUAL/PRESSURE COOK: **2 MINUTES LOW PRESSURE**

RELEASE: **QUICK**

TOTAL TIME: **15 MINUTES**

I never had mulled wine until I went to Germany a few years ago, but I instantly fell in love with it. Like Mexican Hot Chocolate (page 128), it takes a classic beverage and bumps it up a level by adding warming spices like cinnamon, cloves, and star anise. This is a festive drink that I love to serve to celebrate the winter holidays.

1. In the pressure-cooker pot, combine the wine, honey, orange, cinnamon stick, and star anise. Close and lock the lid.
2. Select the Manual/Pressure Cook setting and cook for 2 minutes at low pressure. When cooking is complete, quick release the pressure.
3. Switch the pressure cooker to the Keep Warm setting, and enjoy the wine throughout the evening.

1 (750-milliliter) bottle
  red wine

¼ cup honey

1 orange, sliced

1 cinnamon stick

1 whole star anise

SUBSTITUTION: Don't have star anise? No problem. For a similar but slightly different flavor, substitute 2 whole cloves for the star anise.

Spicy Chocolate Cake

Serves 6 to 8

PREP TIME: **15 MINUTES**

SAUTÉ: **5 MINUTES**

MANUAL/PRESSURE COOK: **15 MINUTES HIGH PRESSURE**

RELEASE: **QUICK**

TOTAL TIME: **45 MINUTES**

This recipe is adapted from a Mexican chocolate brownie recipe that I included in my first cookbook, *La Latina*. High-quality dark chocolate (70 percent cocoa solids or higher) is key to getting the rich flavor you want here. This cake is flourless (and gluten-free), so it's extra rich and fudgy. A pinch of cayenne adds just a little kick that really makes it stand out, but you can skip it if you're cooking for the kids. You won't believe this cake was made in a pressure cooker!

1. Spray a 7-inch springform pan with cooking spray. Cut a parchment paper round to fit in the pan and place it inside the pan. Set aside.

2. In the pressure-cooker pot, pour 1 cup of water and set to Sauté.

3. In a medium bowl that will fit inside the pressure-cooker pot, combine the chocolate chips and butter. Set the bowl inside the pressure-cooker pot and stir regularly until the chocolate and butter are melted, about 5 minutes. Once melted, carefully remove the bowl from the cooker and set aside.

4. Place the egg yolks in a small bowl and the whites in a large bowl. Add 2 tablespoons of sugar to the yolks and beat until pale in color, about 3 minutes. Set aside.

Cooking spray

1 cup dark chocolate chips or chopped dark chocolate

4 tablespoons unsalted butter

3 large eggs, separated

4 tablespoons sugar, divided

Pinch cayenne pepper

Walnuts, chopped (optional)

TECHNIQUE: Parchment paper is an endlessly useful kitchen supply to have on hand. It can help prevent messes and make cleanup easy for any number of kitchen tasks. Here it prevents the cake from sticking to the bottom of the pan and allows you to transfer the cake to a serving tray easily.

5. Beat the egg whites with the remaining 2 tablespoons of sugar until stiff peaks form, about 5 minutes.

6. Add the egg yolks to the melted chocolate and whisk to combine. Mix in the cayenne and walnuts (if using). Carefully fold in the egg whites until incorporated.

7. Pour the mixture into the prepared pan and cover with aluminum foil. Place the trivet in the cooker, and lower the pan onto the trivet. Close and lock the lid.

8. Select the Manual/Pressure Cook setting and cook for 15 minutes at high pressure. When cooking is complete, quick release the pressure. Carefully unlock and remove the lid.

9. Carefully remove the cake and foil, and cool at room temperature for 10 minutes. Remove the parchment paper and enjoy.

Salsa Verde, *page 138*

CHAPTER 8

Staples

Making stocks, sauces, and other staples is one place where the electric pressure cooker really comes in handy. You can cook large batches of broth to stash in the freezer, and salsas, sauces, and marinades to keep in the fridge.

The Instant Pot, Cosori, and Power Pressure Cooker XL all include Soup and/or Broth buttons.

Chicken Stock

Makes about 1½ quarts

PREP TIME: **10 MINUTES**

MANUAL/PRESSURE COOK: **20 MINUTES HIGH PRESSURE**

RELEASE: **NATURAL**

TOTAL TIME: **1 HOUR**

I make a very simple stock, which I use as a base for soups and sauces. After the stock is made, I shred the meat and use that for things like Sofrito Chicken Stew (page 86), Shredded Chicken Marinara (page 87), or Shredded Chicken in Avocado Salad (page 88), so I get multiple meals from this humble stock.

1. Thinly slice the white part of the leek and place the slices in a bowl of water for 15 minutes. Skim the pieces out of the bowl and pat dry with a paper towel. Wash the dark green leek leaves (if using) in the same bowl or under a faucet, cleaning thoroughly. Tie the leaves together with butcher's twine.

2. In the pressure-cooker pot, add the chicken, white leek slices, onion, garlic, celery, and leek leaves or herb stems tied with butcher's twine. Cover the chicken with water. Close and lock the lid.

3. Use the Manual/Pressure Cook setting and cook for 20 minutes at high pressure. When cooking is complete, allow the pressure to release naturally. Unlock and carefully remove the lid.

4. Remove the leek leaves or herb stems and discard.

5. Remove the chicken carefully (it will be falling off the bone) and shred with two forks. Pack the shredded chicken into airtight storage containers and refrigerate for 3 to 4 days or freeze for up to 1 month.

6. Using a sieve set over a bowl, strain the stock and let cool for about 30 minutes. Divide the stock into airtight containers and refrigerate for 3 to 4 days or freeze for up to 1 month.

1 leek, white part only

Leek leaves (dark green), or parsley or cilantro stems, tied with butcher's twine so you can easily remove them

2 pounds whole chicken, butchered (ideally with bones and skin, to add more flavor)

1 onion, roughly chopped

4 garlic cloves, smashed

2 celery stalks, roughly chopped

Fresh parsley or cilantro leaves, chopped, for garnish (optional)

FREEZER TIP: Making this chicken stock and shredded meat is a great way to plan ahead for busy days when there's not much time for cooking. When packaging the meat or broth to freeze, be sure to use freezer-safe storage containers. Divide the broth and meat into portions that you regularly use in recipes, such as 1 or 2 cups, so that you don't have to thaw and divide the entire batch of stock or meat later.

INGREDIENT TIP: Because their leaves grow in tight layers, leeks tend to have a lot of dirt trapped inside them and therefore require extra-thorough cleaning.

Fish Stock

Makes approximately 2 cups

PREP TIME: **5 MINUTES**

MANUAL/PRESSURE COOK: **25 MINUTES HIGH PRESSURE**

RELEASE: **NATURAL**

TOTAL TIME: **50 MINUTES**

I use this simple but flavorful stock to make Shrimp Chupe (page 64) or Arroz Negro (page 112). I also like to keep a jar of this in my fridge for a nutritious snack. Just heat it up and add a squeeze of lime juice and a few sprigs of cilantro.

1. In the pressure-cooker pot, add the fish bones, onion, celery stalk, parsley stems, peppercorns, and ½ cup water. Close and lock the lid.

2. Select the Manual/Pressure Cook setting and cook for 25 minutes at high pressure. When cooking is complete, allow the pressure to release naturally. Unlock and carefully remove the lid.

3. Using a large sieve set over a bowl, strain the stock and let it cool for about 30 minutes. Divide the strained stock into freezer-safe storage containers and refrigerate for 3 or 4 days or freeze for up to 1 month.

2 pounds fish heads
  and bones

1 onion, roughly chopped

1 celery stalk

1 bunch parsley stems

1 teaspoon whole black
  peppercorns

TECHNIQUE: I only add ½ cup of water because the fish will release a lot of water while it cooks, making a super-flavorful stock.

Vegetable Stock

Makes 3 cups

PREP TIME: **5 MINUTES**

MANUAL/PRESSURE COOK: **20 MINUTES HIGH PRESSURE**

RELEASE: **NATURAL**

TOTAL TIME: **40 MINUTES**

This simple vegetable stock can be turned into any number of vegetarian soups or sauces, or used as a flavorful cooking liquid for vegetables. As with meat stocks, I like to keep extra vegetable stock in the freezer for easy meals.

1. In the pressure-cooker pot, add the onions, celery, carrot, garlic, peppercorns, and 3 cups water. Close and lock the lid.

2. Select the Manual/Pressure Cook setting and cook for 20 minutes at high pressure. When cooking is complete, allow the pressure to release naturally. Unlock and carefully remove the lid.

3. Using a large sieve, strain the stock and let it cool. Divide the strained stock into airtight storage containers and refrigerate for 3 or 4 days or freeze for up to 1 month.

2 onions, halved

2 celery stalks, cut in thirds

1 medium carrot, halved

3 garlic cloves, peeled and smashed

1 teaspoon whole black peppercorns

FREEZER TIP: You can also freeze the stock in an ice-cube tray for small portions that you can just toss into dishes as needed for a bit of extra flavor. Once the tray is frozen, pop the stock cubes out and place them in a freezer-safe storage bag for up to 1 month.

Salsa Roja

Makes 2½ cups

PREP TIME: **5 MINUTES**

SAUTÉ: **5 MINUTES**

MANUAL/PRESSURE COOK: **1 MINUTE HIGH PRESSURE**

RELEASE: **QUICK**

TOTAL TIME: **15 MINUTES**

2 cups cherry tomatoes

**1 serrano chile,
   stem removed**

1 garlic clove, peeled

**2 cups Chicken Stock
   (page 134)**

Flaky sea salt

You'll want to keep a batch of this simple yet flavorful sauce in your fridge at all times. It's a spicy red sauce originating in Mexico, where it's used on just about everything. I used to make it the traditional way: standing over the stove top, waiting for the tomatoes, chiles, and garlic to char, watching it constantly to prevent burning, then mashing it in a *molcajete* (mortar and pestle). Making it in the electric pressure cooker is much easier. The trick is cooking it long enough that the tomatoes develop blackened spots—that's how the sauce gets its trademark smokiness. Use this salsa on carnitas (see Shredded Pork, page 101), Huevos Rancheros Casserole (page 24), tacos, or burritos.

OPTION: If you prefer a smooth salsa over a chunky one, or if the chile and garlic clove aren't mostly dissolved, pulse in a blender or use an immersion blender right in the pot to achieve the desired consistency.

1. Select the Sauté function and combine the tomatoes, serrano, and garlic in the pressure-cooker pot. Sauté until charred, stirring occasionally, about 5 minutes.

2. Add the stock and deglaze, scraping any browned bits off the bottom of the pot. Stir well. Close and lock the lid.

3. Select the Manual/Pressure Cook setting and cook for 1 minute at high pressure. When the cooking is complete, quick release the pressure. Unlock and carefully remove the lid. Season with sea salt.

Salsa Verde

Makes 1 cup

PREP TIME: **10 MINUTES**

MANUAL/PRESSURE COOK: **5 MINUTES HIGH PRESSURE**

RELEASE: **QUICK**

TOTAL TIME: **20 MINUTES**

This sauce is also a common staple in Mexico, similar to Salsa Roja (page 137). It combines tangy tomatillos and cilantro with chiles, garlic, and onion for a zingy sauce that's delicious with scrambled or fried eggs, on fish tacos, or folded into shredded chicken for Chicken Chilaquiles (page 94). You can store this sauce in the refrigerator for a couple of weeks, so make a large batch. You'll find plenty of ways to use it.

1. In the pressure-cooker pot, add the tomatillos, onion, cilantro, serrano, garlic, and ½ cup water. Close and lock the lid.

2. Select the Manual/Pressure Cook setting and cook for 5 minutes at high pressure. When cooking is complete, quick release the pressure. Unlock and carefully remove the lid. Season with sea salt.

3. Transfer to an airtight container and store refrigerated for up to 2 weeks.

½ pound tomatillos, husked and rinsed

1 small onion, roughly chopped

1 cup roughly chopped cilantro

1 serrano chile, stemmed and deseeded

1 garlic clove, peeled

Flaky sea salt

OPTION: If you prefer a smooth salsa, transfer the finished salsa to a blender or use an immersion blender in the pot and pulse the salsa to achieve the desired consistency.

Marinara Sauce

Makes 1½ cups

PREP TIME: **5 MINUTES**

SAUTÉ: **1 MINUTE**

MANUAL/PRESSURE COOK: **5 MINUTES HIGH PRESSURE**

RELEASE: **QUICK**

TOTAL TIME: **15 MINUTES**

This marinara sauce on top of pasta is a perfect, easy vegetarian meal. If you want to make it a bit more filling, add ground beef, lamb, or sweet or spicy Italian sausage. You can also use this sauce as a cooking medium for fish or shellfish or the base for the Bolognese Sauce (page 102).

1. Select the Sauté function and add the olive oil and garlic. Cook briefly, without browning.

2. Add the tomatoes, basil, chili flakes (if using), and oregano (if using). Close and lock the lid.

3. Select Manual/Pressure Cook and cook for 5 minutes at high pressure. When cooking is complete, quick release the pressure. Carefully unlock and remove the lid.

4. Transfer the sauce to an airtight storage container. Refrigerate for up to 1 week or freeze for up to 1 month.

2 tablespoons extra-virgin olive oil

6 garlic cloves, minced

1 (12-ounce) can crushed San Marzano tomatoes

10 fresh basil leaves, left whole

Pinch chili flakes (optional)

½ teaspoon chopped fresh oregano leaves (optional)

OPTION: You can add more chili flakes if you want more heat, or leave them out if you want less heat. Also, if you like your marinara sauce on the sweeter side, add ½ cup chopped carrot, sautéing it before the garlic, then blending the finished sauce until smooth.

Sofrito Base Sauce

Makes 4 cups

PREP TIME: **5 MINUTES**

MANUAL/PRESSURE COOK: **5 MINUTES HIGH PRESSURE**

RELEASE: **QUICK**

TOTAL TIME: **15 MINUTES**

Sofrito sauce is the foundation of many Latin dishes, and several variations of it exist. My grandmother used just garlic, onion, and peppers for her sofrito. I like to add tomato purée as well. This sauce is a staple in my kitchen; I use it as the starting point for many dishes, including Shakshuka-Style Baked Eggs (page 26), Sofrito Chicken Stew (page 86), Carne Mechada (page 98), and many others.

1. Thinly slice the white part of the leek (if using) and place the slices in a bowl of water for 15 minutes. Skim the pieces out of the bowl and pat dry with a paper towel.

2. In the pressure-cooker pot, add the olive oil, red pepper, onion, and white leek slices (if using). Select the Sauté setting and cook, stirring regularly, until the onion is translucent.

3. Add the garlic, and continue to cook for 1 minute.

4. Add the tomato paste, mix well, and cook for about 1 minute. Add the tomato purée and a pinch of salt. Close and lock the lid.

5. Select the Manual/Pressure Cook setting and cook for 5 minutes at high pressure. When cooking is complete, quick release the pressure. Carefully unlock and remove the lid.

6. Transfer the sauce to an airtight storage container. Refrigerate for up to 1 week or freeze for up to 3 months.

1 leek, white part only (optional)

2 tablespoons extra-virgin olive oil

1 red bell pepper, finely diced or pulsed in a food processor

1 onion, finely diced or pulsed in a food processor

2 garlic cloves, minced

1 tablespoon tomato paste

1 (24.5-ounce) jar tomato purée passata

Salt

TECHNIQUE: Take care not to overseason the sauce, because it's a base for other dishes that will include their own seasoning.

INGREDIENT TIP: Because their leaves grow in tight layers, leeks tend to have a lot of dirt trapped inside them and therefore require extra-thorough cleaning.

Chimichurri

Makes 1 cup

PREP TIME: **5 MINUTES**

Chimichurri is an uncooked sauce (salsa) made from fresh herbs, olive oil, and garlic, and it's a staple in the cuisines of Argentina and Uruguay. It's a quick way to add bright, fresh flavor to just about anything, especially chicken, fish, or meat. Add it to cooked meat or vegetables as a finishing sauce, or use it as a marinade.

In a small mixing bowl or blender, mix together the olive oil, parsley, lemon juice, oregano, garlic, and red pepper flakes. Season with salt. Let rest for about 30 minutes before serving.

½ cup extra-virgin olive oil

½ cup finely chopped fresh flat-leaf Italian parsley

¼ cup lemon juice, white vinegar, or sherry vinegar

1 tablespoon dried oregano, lightly crushed

2 garlic cloves, finely minced

Pinch red pepper flakes

Flaky sea salt

OPTION: To turn this chimichurri into a mint chimichurri, add ½ cup very finely chopped fresh mint and 1 tablespoon of finely chopped rosemary. Season with flaky sea salt and freshly ground black pepper.

Pesto Sauce

Makes ½ cup

PREP TIME: **10 MINUTES**

This classic Italian sauce made of fresh basil, garlic, and olive oil is, of course, delicious on pasta, but it can also be used in so many other ways. I like to stir it into rice or use it as a sauce for fish or meat. It also makes a great pizza sauce in place of the more common tomato-based sauce.

In a blender, combine the basil, parsley, olive oil, garlic clove, salt, and black pepper. Process until smooth. Store in an airtight container in the refrigerator for up to 1 week.

1 cup lightly packed
  fresh basil leaves,
  coarsely chopped
½ cup lightly packed
  fresh parsley leaves,
  coarsely chopped
½ cup extra-virgin olive oil
1 garlic clove, crushed
½ teaspoon salt
Pinch freshly ground
  black pepper

FREEZER: Pesto can also be frozen in small portion sizes for easy additions to recipes. Freeze pesto in ice-cube trays, then transfer the cubes to a freezer-safe storage bag and freeze for up to 3 months. Add a cube or two to sauces, pizza, and pasta dishes for a quick and easy flavor boost.

Cuban Mojo Sauce

Makes 1 cup

PREP TIME: **5 MINUTES**

SAUTÉ: **2 MINUTE**

MANUAL/PRESSURE COOK: **3 MINUTES HIGH PRESSURE**

RELEASE: **QUICK**

TOTAL TIME: **15 MINUTES**

6 cloves fresh garlic, peeled

1 cup olive oil

½ cup orange juice

½ cup lime juice

½ teaspoon sea salt, plus
additional for seasoning

Fresh parsley or oregano,
chopped (optional)

INGREDIENTS: Add this sauce
to your favorite protein or
vegetable and sprinkle some
freshly chopped parsley or
oregano on top if desired.

Mojo is a citrus- and garlic-infused sauce that goes well with EVERYTHING—especially Vaca Frita (page 99), Shredded Pork (page 101), and Whole Chicken (page 84). It's a very diverse sauce, good for marinating or just as a dip. I love making this sauce in the electric pressure cooker, because it's extra easy and safe. Traditionally you have to mash the garlic on a mortar and pestle and the citrus juice has a tendency to splatter when it's added to the hot oil—but none of that is a worry with this electric pressure cooker version!

1. Add the olive oil to the pot, and select the Sauté setting on high. Once hot, add the garlic and cook until slightly brown, about 2 minutes.

2. Add the orange juice, lime juice, and salt. Secure the lid and pressure cook on high for 3 minutes.

3. When the pressure cooking is complete, use the quick release and remove the lid. Mash the garlic with a fork and stir to combine. Season to taste with sea salt, and stir in the fresh parsley or oregano (if desired).

Homemade Mixed Berry Sauce

Makes 4 cups

PREP TIME: **5 MINUTES**

MANUAL/PRESSURE COOK: **1 MINUTE HIGH PRESSURE**

RELEASE: **NATURAL**

TOTAL TIME: **20 MINUTES**

This simple fruit sauce makes a perfect topping for ice cream, frozen yogurt, or cheesecake. I also love it stirred into yogurt, oatmeal, or breakfast porridge. You can use any combination of frozen berries you like, or even just stick with one type, such as raspberries or boysenberries.

1. In a pressure-cooker pot, combine the mixed berries, orange liqueur or juice, and orange zest. Close and lock the lid.

2. Select the Manual/Pressure Cook setting and cook for 1 minute at high pressure. When cooking is complete, allow the pressure to release naturally. Carefully unlock and remove the lid.

3. Use a slotted spoon to transfer the berries to a storage container. For a juicier sauce, mix in some of the juice from the pot. If desired, use an immersion blender (or transfer to a regular blender) to purée the berries for a smooth sauce. Store in the refrigerator for up to 5 days.

4 cups frozen mixed berry medley, thawed

1 tablespoon orange liqueur (such as triple sec) or orange juice

½ teaspoon grated orange zest

TECHNIQUE: The reason to use natural release in this recipe is to prevent any berry sauce from splattering out of the steam-release valve. Sauces like this are prone to splattering, so to save yourself the cleanup later, let it rest for about 15 minutes after cooking to release its pressure.

Apple Compote

Makes 3 cups

PREP TIME: **5 MINUTES**

MANUAL/PRESSURE COOK: **1 MINUTE HIGH PRESSURE**

RELEASE: **QUICK**

TOTAL TIME: **20 MINUTES**

I don't know about you, but I usually buy too much of any ingredient that's in season, especially apples. When I end up with a bunch of apples, I like to turn them into a compote. It's naturally sweet, making it a perfect topping for French toast, yogurt, Butternut Squash and Coconut Porridge (page 33), or Challah Bread Pudding (page 37). Drizzle a bit of honey or maple syrup on top if you like.

1. In the pressure-cooker pot, combine the apples, ginger, cinnamon stick, nutmeg, lemon juice, and lemon zest.

2. Select the Manual/Pressure Cook setting and cook for 1 minute at high pressure. When cooking is complete, quick release the pressure. Unlock and carefully remove the lid.

3. Cool for about 5 minutes. Using a slotted spoon, transfer the apple compote to an airtight storage container. Discard the juices left behind in the pot.

6 **Red Delicious or Gala apples, cored, peeled, and cut into 1-inch pieces**

¼ **teaspoon grated fresh ginger**

1 **cinnamon stick**

Pinch nutmeg

Juice of 1 lemon

Zest of ½ lemon

MAKE-AHEAD TIP:
This compote will last for up to 1 week in the fridge.

Electric Pressure Cooking Time Charts

The following charts provide approximate cook times used for a variety of foods in a 6-quart electric pressure cooker like the Instant Pot. Larger electric pressure cookers may need a little extra time to cook. To begin, you may want to cook for a minute or two less than the times listed; you can always simmer foods at natural pressure to finish cooking.

Keep in mind that these times apply to the foods when partially submerged in water (or broth), steamed, or cooked alone. However, the cooking times for a given food may differ when it's used in different recipes, because of additional ingredients or cooking liquids, a different release method than the one listed here, and so on.

For any foods labeled "natural release," allow at least 15 minutes of natural pressure release before quick releasing any remaining pressure.

Beans and Legumes

When cooking a pound or more of beans, it's best to use low pressure and increase the cooking time by a minute or two, because larger amounts at high pressure are prone to foaming. If you have less than a pound of beans, high pressure is fine. A little oil in the cooking liquid will reduce foaming as well.

Unless a shorter release time is indicated, let the pressure release naturally for at least 15 minutes, after which any remaining pressure can be quick released.

	MINUTES UNDER PRESSURE UNSOAKED	MINUTES UNDER PRESSURE SOAKED IN SALTED WATER	PRESSURE	RELEASE
Black beans	22	10	High	Natural
	25	12	Low	
Black-eyed peas	12	5	High	Natural for 8 minutes, then quick
	15	7	Low	
Cannellini beans	25	8	High	Natural
	28	10	Low	
Chickpeas (garbanzo beans)	18	3	High	Natural for 3 minutes, then quick
	20	4	Low	
Kidney beans	25	8	High	Natural
	28	10	Low	
Lentils	10	Not recommended	High	Quick
Lima beans	15	4	High	Natural for 5 minutes, then quick
	18	5	Low	
Navy beans	18	8	High	Natural
	20	10	Low	
Pinto beans	25	10	High	Natural
	28	12	Low	
Soybeans, dried	25	12	High	Natural
	28	14	Low	
Soybeans, fresh (edamame)	1	Not recommended	High	Quick
Split peas (unsoaked)	5 (firm peas) to 8 (soft peas)	Not recommended	High	Natural

Grains

To prevent foaming, it's best to rinse grains thoroughly before cooking, or include a small amount of butter or oil with the cooking liquid. Unless a shorter release time is indicated, let the pressure release naturally for at least 15 minutes, after which any remaining pressure can be quick released.

	LIQUID PER 1 CUP OF GRAIN	MINUTES UNDER PRESSURE	PRESSURE	RELEASE
Arborio (or other medium-grain) rice	1½ cups	6	High	Quick
Barley, pearled	2½ cups	10	High	Natural
Brown rice, long grain	1½ cups	13	High	Natural for 10 minutes, then quick
Brown rice, medium grain	1½ cups	6–8	High	Natural
Buckwheat	1¾ cups	2–4	High	Natural
Farro, pearled	2 cups	6–8	High	Natural
Farro, whole grain	3 cups	22–24	High	Natural
Oats, rolled	3 cups	3–4	High	Quick
Oats, steel-cut	4 cups	12	High	Natural
Quinoa	2 cups	2	High	Quick
Wheat berries	2 cups	30	High	Natural for 10 minutes, then quick
White rice, long grain	1½ cups	3	High	Quick
Wild rice	2½ cups	18–20	High	Natural

Meat

Except as noted, the times below are for braised meats—that is, meats that are seared before pressure-cooking and partially submerged in liquid. Unless a shorter release time is indicated, let the pressure release naturally for at least 15 minutes, after which any remaining pressure can be quick released.

	MINUTES UNDER PRESSURE	PRESSURE	RELEASE
Beef, shoulder (chuck), 2" chunks	20	High	Natural for 10 minutes
Beef, shoulder (chuck) roast (2 lb.)	35	High	Natural
Beef, bone-in short ribs	40	High	Natural
Beef, flat iron steak, cut into ½" strips	1	Low	Quick
Beef, sirloin steak, cut into ½" strips	1	Low	Quick
Lamb, shanks	40	High	Natural
Lamb, shoulder, 2" chunks	35	High	Natural
Pork, back ribs (steamed)	30	High	Quick
Pork, shoulder, 2" chunks	20	High	Natural
Pork, shoulder roast (2 lb.)	25	High	Natural
Pork, smoked sausage, ½" slices	20	High	Quick
Pork, spare ribs (steamed)	20	High	Quick
Pork, tenderloin	4	Low	Quick

Poultry

Except as noted, the times below are for poultry that is partially submerged in liquid. Unless a shorter release time is indicated, let the pressure release naturally for at least 15 minutes, after which any remaining pressure can be quick released.

	MINUTES UNDER PRESSURE	PRESSURE	RELEASE
Chicken breast, bone-in (steamed)	8	Low	Natural for 5 minutes
Chicken breast, boneless (steamed)	5	Low	Natural for 8 minutes
Chicken thigh, bone-in	15	High	Natural for 10 minutes
Chicken thigh, boneless	8	High	Natural for 10 minutes
Chicken thigh, boneless, 1"–2" pieces	5	High	Quick
Chicken, whole (seared on all sides)	12–14	Low	Natural for 8 minutes
Duck quarters, bone-in	35	High	Quick
Turkey breast, tenderloin (12 oz.) (steamed)	5	Low	Natural for 8 minutes
Turkey thigh, bone-in	30	High	Natural

Seafood

All times are for steamed fish and shellfish.

	MINUTES UNDER PRESSURE	PRESSURE	RELEASE
Clams	2	High	Quick
Halibut, fresh (1" thick)	3	High	Quick
Large shrimp, frozen	1	Low	Quick
Mussels	1	High	Quick
Salmon, fresh (1" thick)	5	Low	Quick
Tilapia or cod, fresh	1	Low	Quick
Tilapia or cod, frozen	3	Low	Quick

Vegetables

The cooking method for all the following vegetables is steaming; if the vegetables are cooked in liquid, the times may vary. Green vegetables will be crisp-tender; root vegetables will be soft. Unless a shorter release time is indicated, let the pressure release naturally for at least 15 minutes, after which any remaining pressure can be quick released.

	PREP	MINUTES UNDER PRESSURE	PRESSURE	RELEASE
Acorn squash	Halved	9	High	Quick
Artichokes, large	Whole	15	High	Quick
Beets	Quartered if large; halved if small	9	High	Natural
Broccoli	Cut into florets	1	Low	Quick
Brussels sprouts	Halved	2	High	Quick
Butternut squash	Peeled, ½" chunks	8	High	Quick
Cabbage	Sliced	5	High	Quick
Carrots	½"–1" slices	2	High	Quick
Cauliflower	Whole	6	High	Quick
Cauliflower	Cut into florets	1	Low	Quick
Green beans	Cut in half or thirds	1	Low	Quick
Potatoes, large russet (for mashing)	Quartered	8	High	Natural for 8 minutes, then quick
Potatoes, red	Whole if less than 1½" across; halved if larger	4	High	Quick
Spaghetti squash	Halved lengthwise	7	High	Quick
Sweet potatoes	Halved lengthwise	8	High	Natural

The Dirty Dozen &
the Clean Fifteen™

A nonprofit environmental watchdog organization called Environmental Working Group (EWG) looks at data supplied by the U.S. Department of Agriculture (USDA) and the Food and Drug Administration (FDA) about pesticide residues. Each year it compiles a list of the best and worst pesticide loads found in commercial crops. You can use these lists to decide which fruits and vegetables to buy organic to minimize your exposure to pesticides and which produce is considered safe enough to buy conventionally. This does not mean they are pesticide-free, though, so wash these fruits and vegetables thoroughly.

DIRTY DOZEN

- Apples
- Celery
- Cherries
- Grapes
- Nectarines
- Peaches
- Pears
- Potatoes
- Spinach
- Strawberries
- Sweet bell peppers
- Tomatoes

In addition to the Dirty Dozen, the EWG added one type of produce contaminated with highly toxic organophosphate insecticides:

- Hot peppers

CLEAN FIFTEEN

- Asparagus
- Avocados
- Cabbage
- Cantaloupes (domestic)
- Cauliflower
- Eggplants
- Grapefruits
- Honeydew
- Kiwis
- Mangos
- Onions
- Papayas
- Pineapples
- Sweet corn
- Sweet peas (frozen)

Measurement Conversions

VOLUME EQUIVALENTS (Liquid)

U.S. STANDARD	U.S. STANDARD (OUNCES)	METRIC (APPROXIMATE)
2 tablespoons	1 fl. oz.	30 mL
¼ cup	2 fl. oz.	60 mL
½ cup	4 fl. oz.	120 mL
1 cup	8 fl. oz.	240 mL
1½ cups	12 fl. oz	355 mL
2 cups or 1 pint	16 fl. oz.	475 mL
4 cups or 1 quart	32 fl. oz.	1 L
1 gallon	128 fl. oz.	4 L

OVEN TEMPERATURES

FAHRENHEIT (F)	CELSIUS (C) (APPROXIMATE)
250°F	120°C
300°F	150°C
325°F	165°C
350°F	180°C
375°F	190°C
400°F	200°C
425°F	220°C
450°F	230°C

VOLUME EQUIVALENTS (Dry)

U.S. STANDARD	METRIC (APPROXIMATE)
⅛ teaspoon	0.5 mL
¼ teaspoon	1 mL
½ teaspoon	2 mL
¾ teaspoon	4 mL
1 teaspoon	5 mL
1 tablespoon	15 mL
¼ cup	59 mL
⅓ cup	79 mL
½ cup	118 mL
⅔ cup	156 mL
¾ cup	177 mL
1 cup	235 mL
2 cups or 1 pint	475 mL
3 cups	700 mL
4 cups or 1 quart	1 L

WEIGHT EQUIVALENTS

U.S. STANDARD	METRIC (APPROXIMATE)
½ ounce	15 g
1 ounce	30 g
2 ounces	60 g
4 ounces	115 g
8 ounces	225 g
12 ounces	340 g
16 ounces or 1 pound	455 g

References

Presilla, Maricel E. *Gran Cocina Latina*.
New York: W. W. Norton & Company,
2012.

Ramirez, Grace. *La Latina*. Auckland:
Penguin Random House New Zealand
Limited, 2015.

Recipe Index

Index

Acknowledgments

Thank you to my family and my tribe—you all know who you are. It takes a village to make a book come to life, and I couldn't be more grateful for my dream team.

Thank you to Melissa Tung, Adela Smith, Helen Muñoz, and Robin Donovan for all your hard work. I couldn't have done it without you ladies.

Thank you to Kim Suarez for considering me for this passion project. I had an amazing time making this cookbook, and now I'm more obsessed than ever with the electric pressure cooker.

Thank you to the Callisto Media team. You guys have been a pleasure to work with.

With love and gratitude,

—Grace Ramirez

About the Author

Grace Ramirez is an international chef with a degree from the prestigious French Culinary Institute. Born in Miami but raised in Venezuela, her culinary style combines soul food with her own brand of chic, reflecting her roots, inspirations, and passion. She is the host of Cooking Channel's *Gooey* and *Food Network LATAM: Destino con Sabor*.

Grace started her journey as a contestant on *Masterchef USA*, where she was selected out of 60,000 applicants and trained with Gordon Ramsey. Shortly after the show and culinary school, she landed in New Zealand, where she quickly rose to become one of the country's most beloved celebrity chefs. She is currently an expert judge on one of NZ's highest-rated shows, *My Kitchen Rules*, which airs throughout NZ, Asia, and the UK.

Before launching her own platform, Grace worked with some of the world's biggest media companies, such as Viacom/Nickelodeon, MTV, and Food Network, where she was a producer on *Throwdown with Bobby Flay*.

She has appeared on *The Chew*, Telemundo's Emmy Award-winning show *El Nuevo Día*, Univision, and many more. She has been featured in *Food52* and *Cherry Bombe*. Grace lives in New York City.

CPSIA information can be obtained
at www.ICGtesting.com
Printed in the USA
BVHW06s1444190518
516611BV00003B/4/P